FAST EDDIE

EDDIE MAHER

BLINK

bringing you closer

Published by Blink Publishing
3.08, The Plaza,
535 Kings Road,
Chelsea Harbour,
London, SW10 0SZ

www.blinkpublishing.co.uk

facebook.com/blinkpublishing
twitter.com/blinkpublishing

Hardback – 978-1-91127-435-3
Trade Paperback – 978-1-91127-436-0
Ebook – 978-1-91127-437-7

A CIP catalogue of this book is available from the British Library.

Cover design by Nathan Balsom
Typeset by EnvyDesignLtd
Printed and bound by Clays Ltd, St. Ives Plc

1 3 5 7 9 10 8 6 4 2

Papers used by Blink Publishing are natural, recyclable products made from
wood grown in sustainable forests. The manufacturing processes conform to the
environmental regulations of the country of origin.

Every reasonable effort has been made to trace copyright holders of material
reproduced in this book, but if any have been inadvertently overlooked the publishers
would be glad to hear from them.

Blink Publishing is an imprint of the Bonnier Publishing Group
www.bonnierpublishing.co.uk

To my wife and trusted best friend, Deborah. You have always been there for me through thick and thin and I couldn't be without you my DAB. Thank you for putting up with my crap throughout the years and for being the rock that supports our family.

CONTENTS

PROLOGUE MIRROR, SIGNAL, MAN AWOL   IX

CHAPTER 1 EDDIE KID   1

CHAPTER 2 EDDIE GET YOUR GUN   13

CHAPTER 3 LONDON'S BURNING   29

CHAPTER 4 TIME, GENTLEMEN, PLEASE   45

CHAPTER 5 IN THE 'COR   59

CHAPTER 6 THE SET-UP   67

CHAPTER 7 HEIST   81

CHAPTER 8 GETAWAY   93

CHAPTER 9 DEBBIE IN THE USA   109

CHAPTER 10 ACES HIGH   121

CHAPTER 11 REV MAHER   133

CHAPTER 12   TAKING THE MICHAEL   145

CHAPTER 13   KEEP ON TRUCKIN'   157

CHAPTER 14   RESPECTABLE ME   169

CHAPTER 15   AVERAGE JOE   183

CHAPTER 16   EVERYTHING UNRAVELS   195

CHAPTER 17   BUSTED   209

CHAPTER 18   NOT-SO-FAST EDDIE   221

CHAPTER 19   HOMEWARD BOUND   241

CHAPTER 20   BANG-UP   255

CHAPTER 21   THE FINAL FURLONG   273

EPILOGUE   FREEDOM, OF SORTS   281

ACKNOWLEDGEMENTS   289

MIRROR, SIGNAL, MAN AWOL

In every life there are turning points; the little decisions or actions that affect the course of the rest of your life and the lives of those around you. They may seem irrelevant at the time. They can be the smallest things that you don't even think about, like turning left instead of right or having a beer instead of going home. Every action, they say, has a reaction, every cause has an effect. Sometimes we decide things, or do something, and the effect is minimal. My decision to have a curry for tea tonight is unlikely to alter the course of my life or yours for that matter – unless it's a dodgy dinner from the takeaway down the road with a one-star hygiene rating. Other decisions may seem innocuous at the time but, like rocks thrown in a pond, they send ripples out that spread on for years and affect everything that comes after.

FAST EDDIE

At 9.30 am on 22 January 1993, I was parked in front of Lloyds Bank in dreary Felixstowe, Suffolk, getting ready to throw the biggest metaphorical rock into the pond of my life. It's fair to say I was crapping myself. Outside the world was going about its usual business. Felixstowe was an unremarkable grey and faded sea port. It smelt of ozone, diesel and decline. No one ambling around my vehicle had any idea I was about to put the town on the map: not the commuters walking past, the mums on the way back from the school run or the pensioners waiting out their last days in the bracing sea breeze. Even my colleague that day, the comically named Peter Bunn, didn't have a clue what was about to transpire.

Subsequent headlines will have you believe that what happened that day in the high street was full of drama, tension and squealing tyres. The truth is that the action I took was a little more mundane. All I did was slip the vehicle into first and pull away from the side of the kerb. It was all very simple. The events leading up to that pivotal moment had been a lot more dramatic and things were about to get much spicier – but more of that later.

For the moment, there I was, painfully aware that what I was about to do would change everything for me, my loved ones and for everyone around me, including the hapless Mr Bunn.

Ten minutes before this unremarkable event with its profound consequences, Peter and I had pulled up outside the bank. We'd met at work that morning, made a bit of small talk and loaded up the van we were driving. It was a delivery van. We were, to all intents and purposes, delivery drivers. It wasn't a career I'd chosen and, to be honest, it wasn't a job I particularly wanted or enjoyed. I was a fireman by vocation and had been a fireman for 11 years before I was forced out of the service I loved through injury. Before that I'd spent a spell as a sharpshooter in the army, had completed two tours of Northern Ireland and, after being pensioned from the fire brigade, had also had a disastrous spell as a landlord that ended in a firebombing. More of that later, too.

I had my partner Debbie and a three-year-old son Lee to support and life was a struggle. I had some debts and I wanted a decent life for my family. I had always been a grafter and when I saw the delivery job advertised, I applied and was offered the position. It helped that I had previous experience of delivering the commodity that was piled in the back of my Securicor van that day. Cash. Lots and lots of cash. Over one million pounds of it, neatly wrapped in opaque cellophane and stuffed into black canvas kit bags that could be piled up to make convenient seats in the back of the mobile fortress I was driving.

I didn't know how much was in the vehicle. I was on the bank run, the delivery route that included most of the banks and building societies along the Suffolk and Essex coastline. I knew there was a lot of money. There always was on that run. It was a big delivery and we had loaded the cargo ourselves. The bank run was the most valuable cash delivery route out of our depot. It was also one that finished nice and early, which is why I chose to do it. I liked to get home at a reasonable hour so I could spend time with Debbie and Lee. On the day in question, however, my loved ones were away. I'd been forced to send them to the other side of the world for their own safety. They had no idea what was about to go down, they had no idea their lives had been threatened and they had no inkling of the shit-storm I was going to stir up by doing that one simple thing – slipping the van into first gear and driving off with a van-load of someone else's money.

I was contemplating all this while I watched Peter walk to the front door of Lloyds. I knew that at some point that morning, early in the route, I was going to get a signal. I suspected that it would happen during the first drop. There would be no point waiting until half the money had been delivered.

We'd arrived slightly ahead of schedule, which meant that we had to wait in the van until the bank opened. We sat there with the engine running and the heater on because it was cold outside. We chatted about nothing in particular. My mind was elsewhere. Peter was a nice enough bloke. I didn't really know him that well but he seemed decent. I almost felt sorry for him. I knew that if all went according to plan he would be spending a lot of time in police stations over the following days.

I watched through the windscreen and saw one of the bank staff open the door.

'Right,' I said, 'let's get this one done.'

Peter knew the drill. There was a very specific protocol to follow to get the money to the bank. He went to the security airlock in the van and I let him out using the buzzer in the cab. He went and checked the bank was open and gave me the thumbs-up. Then he walked around to the chute at the back where the money would be passed from the driver to the delivery man. I released the inner door in the driver's cabin that led to the chamber at the back of the van where the money was stowed.

Each bank placed an order for a specified amount. The cash was counted and packaged at the depot where it was packed in bags with numbered tags on. The order was written on the delivery sheet for the day and the driver's job was to match the numbers on the sheet with the relevant cash bags in the van and to count out the coins that had also been ordered. There were thousands and thousands of coins on the run. They were also packed in bags. I put the wads of cash in the delivery case, along with the right amount of coins and placed the case in the chute. When I closed that chute inside the van, it opened outside the van where Peter picked up the load and took it to the bank.

I clambered back into the driver's cabin and watched Peter wander across the pavement and through the bank's large wooden doors. My heart was thumping in my chest like a jackhammer. I was convinced that what was going to happen was going to happen there and then. And it did.

As soon as Peter disappeared into the bank a car pulled up alongside me. I recognised it. It was mine. It was being driven by a rat-faced bloke. He was a smartly dressed man, around 50 years old with close-cropped hair. He looked at me and gave me a nod. I took a breath and started the engine.

The irony is that subsequently I was given the name Fast Eddie (the spelling has always been incorrect – I'm actually Eddy with a 'y' but the 'ie' stuck). At that critical moment in time, however, being fast was not an option. I was Careful Driver Eddie. I was Speed Limit Eddie. I was more careful not to be fast than I had ever been in my life because the last thing I needed was to draw attention to myself and the van I was stealing.

The car with the goons in pulled in front of me and I steered the Securicor van with its £1.2 million cash cargo into the road behind it. Together we drove off into the morning traffic. Everyone else continued with their Friday morning. Somewhere across the Atlantic, Debbie and Lee were asleep in a motel room, blissfully unaware that I had just tossed my rock into the pond, so to speak.

The radio in the cab that connected driver to delivery man crackled into life. Peter's confused voice came out of the speaker. He'd done his delivery and was outside the bank.

'Eddie?' he said. 'Eddie... where are you?'

CHAPTER 1

EDDIE KID

'Michael, they're here' may not seem as classic a line as *Moby Dick*'s 'Call me Ishmael' to begin a book, but it is the phrase that sticks in my mind when I think of my story and how I come to be where I am today. It's the phrase that marked the end of my 19-plus years of running and hiding and looking over my shoulder every day. It is the phrase my wife, Debbie, called to me as I sat in the bathroom of our home in the USA when the FBI, immigration and customs enforcement, the police and state troopers came pounding on our door to arrest me.

The other two phrases that symbolise my life are 'How did you get away with it?' and 'Eddie, where's the money?' These are the two questions I always get asked when someone finds out my little secret.

Even now, two decades after I did what I did and following a five-year stretch at Her Majesty's pleasure people still want to know. Why? Possibly because it was seen as the perfect crime – apart from the small fact that I got caught. How was it perfect? Well, the victims were banks and insurance companies and there's not much love lost for them. No one was physically hurt and the police were left scratching their heads and chasing their tails.

The general consensus at the time was that Fast Eddie must be a criminal mastermind, a Scarlet Pimpernel who managed to evade an international police dragnet and outwit the greatest investigative minds in the UK.

Truth, as they say, is stranger than fiction and while the second of the two questions is easy to answer the first question is a longer story. So, what happened to the money? As far as I know, it's long gone. My cut certainly is. It paid for a house in the USA, some fun and games in Vegas, a small single-seater plane, a couple of speedboats and a mid-life retirement that lasted for about seven years until the cash fizzled out and I had to go back to work.

I have no idea what happened to the rest of it. The last I saw of that was when it was being loaded into a Japanese people carrier by a bloke with a broken nose and an interesting array of teeth 20 minutes after I had misappropriated it from Securicor. The bloke turned around, nodded and pissed off. The money was gone to who knows where. I don't even know for sure how much there was. Reports say £1.2 million. Maybe that's true. Maybe someone at Securicor added a bit extra for a better insurance payout. If I had to guess what happened, I would imagine my accomplices either managed to get it out the country somehow and took it somewhere on the continent to wash it clean in a dodgy bank or, alternatively, they slowly spent it over time. A car here, a diamond there, a house, a Rolex, some fancy art work. It soon goes. It may even be buried in a field in Essex somewhere. Sometimes, crooks panic and ditch the haul if the crime gets too much attention. And my little drive-away certainly captured the imagination of the nation. At the time, it was one of the largest heists in British criminal history and for weeks afterwards it made the headlines. On every anniversary for several years, there was a BBC *Crimewatch* reconstruction. Maybe, in the face of such intense interest, the crooks went to ground and got rid of the loot. Who knows?

And so to the more interesting of Fast Eddie's top two most-asked questions. How did I get away with it? The answer to that is really the story of my life and how I went from being a half-cockney, half-Irish skinhead hooligan to becoming an army sharpshooter, a London fireman, Britain's most wanted criminal, a master forger, a reluctant hero and a very able competitive bass fisherman. And to tell that story, I need to start right at the very beginning – in east London in the 1960s where the seeds of my ambiguous attitude to law and order were first sown.

In the East End of my childhood we didn't have heroes but we held people like the Krays and the Richardsons in high regard. They looked after their own and believed in family values.

There wasn't a lot of money to go around and everyone knew that if you wanted to get on in life, you bent the law a little and took opportunities when they presented themselves – just like the gangsters did. Everyone was at it. I grew up around people who had wonky moral compasses. The local copper held a strange place in the community. He wasn't particularly liked but he wasn't hated either. He was begrudgingly tolerated and if you could have one over on him, all the better.

Being a police officer was not a career choice. I can always remember the one person from the neighbourhood who went into the police force – Steve, the little brother of a mate called Jimmy. He loved cop shows on the TV and always rooted for the boys in blue. My allegiances usually swung the other way. When Steve left school he harboured dreams to be a detective like his heroes on the telly and he went into the police force. No one ever spoke to him again. He was the black sheep of the area and his career choice brought shame on his family. Jimmy was mortified. Steve ended up in the regional crime squad.

This was the world me and my 11 siblings grew up in. A post-war, working-class London where concrete council estates were springing up like daisies to replace the ruins left by German bombs and where the best you could do in life was get by. There were opportunities for some but not for people like me and the families on the estate where I lived.

My dad was James Maher, or Jim. He was an Irish Catholic from County Tipperary in Ireland. He emigrated to the UK in the 1940s just after the war. There wasn't much for young men in Eire at that time unless they were farmers and liked potatoes. He liked a spud but he was not green fingered so he came over with a couple of his brothers looking for work and a better way of life. He was a builder and there wasn't much building going on in the emerald isle. But in London post-war reconstruction was going at full pace and he worked on several building sites in the capital and further out in the suburbs. My mum was Elsie Robinson and she came from Bethnal Green in the East End. She was a proper Cockney.

I was born on 2 June 1955, although my actual date of birth was in dispute up until I was 14. When I arrived my parents had so many kids they'd lost track of some of the important dates in the family calendar and it wasn't until my 14th birthday that my actual date of birth was confirmed after one of my sisters looked at my birth certificate. Until then we had been celebrating my birthday on 4 June. That tells you a bit about Maher family life. It was chaotic, but loving.

In my early years, relatives came through the house irregularly. Some would stay for a day or so, some for years. Many were my siblings. Both Mum and Dad had been married before and had children from their previous relationships. I wasn't even aware of this until I was a teenager and it made no difference to me or any of us. My five brothers and six sisters, were as much a part of the family as any of us. Paddy, Jimmy, Rosie and Mary were my dad's kids. Hazel and Barbara were my mum's. Then, together, they had me, Mick, Margaret, Danny, David and Kathleen. I was the third youngest.

There was a generation between the eldest and the youngest and some of my elder siblings had children of their own before I was born. We'd laugh because some of us had uncles and aunts who were younger than we were and nieces and nephews who were older. We were a close family although we were never all in the same house at the same time. There were too many of us to inhabit one space and the age range meant some of my older siblings had already moved out by the time that I came along.

My oldest brother, Paddy, was in the army. It was a career choice a few of us Maher brothers took later in life. Jimmy and Danny joined up for a while too. Paddy was in the Green Jackets and was stationed in the Far East so I didn't meet him for many years. I didn't meet Jimmy until I was older and he arrived unannounced through my bedroom window after getting in a scrape with the law or a gangster – I can't recall which. But I do remember the night of his return.

The sleeping arrangements at home were fairly fluid because of the frequency with which my parents had children. I was in a room with some of my other brothers when I was woken by a foot being firmly planted in my face. I let out a muffled grunt.

'Shorry, mate,' came a slurred voice in the gloom. I was just about to scream out and alert my parents to the intruder when the figure in the dark hushed me and explained, 'Itsh me, your brother, Jimmy. Don't wake Mum, she'll kill me.'

Jimmy's attempts to make a quiet entrance back into the family home after several years away were unsuccessful, however, and Mum and Dad heard the commotion. A light flicked on in the hallway and the bedroom door swung open. Mum stood silhouetted against the landing light, hands on hips. Jimmy duly got an earful before she made him up a bed on the sofa downstairs. The following morning, over breakfast, I was properly introduced.

Before I had been born the family had lived on the outskirts of London at the Fairlop aerodrome site near Ilford for a time, in a make-shift camp of prefab Nissen huts that had been erected for people who had been bombed-out during the war. The camp was next to a rail depot and Dad used to encourage Paddy to climb over the fence to nick the coal stored there for the trains. Everyone mucked in on the camp. As well as Paddy stealing coal, Jimmy – my dad's second son – used to run four miles to the shop every Sunday to get the newspapers. Several of the kids on the camp were given the same task but Jimmy was always the first back. When Dad asked how he did it, Jimmy simply shrugged and explained that he was a good runner. Dad, being Irish, couldn't pass up the opportunity to bet with the neighbours about who had the fastest son. Despite Jimmy's protests, one Sunday several fathers decided to take Dad's wager. Around five boys from the camp set off running to get to the paper shop and back. Given Jimmy's track record, Dad was convinced the race was in the bag and was shocked when Jimmy limped in an hour after the other competitors, red aced and exhausted.

'What happened?' Dad asked.

Jimmy had to admit that he told a few porkies and that every week he'd actually been thumbing a lift with the local baker to the shops in a delivery van.

Dad worked his way up to clerk of works and was well respected in the building game with his uncanny knack of being able to work out complicated maths in his head. After work, he went to the pub every night. He drank Guinness or Jameson whiskey and was a typical Irishman. After the pub his next favourite place was the bookies. Dad worked and Mum stayed at home and looked after the house and the children. She also had a sewing machine and would take in work to earn extra cash.

At the time the family were living in the camp, Dad was working on one of the big estates being built at nearby Newbury Park. He snagged himself one of the best plots of the development, a corner with a larger front and back garden than the others on the street, and built a house for himself. The address was 99 Leyswood Drive, and over the years it became affectionately known simply as '99'. It was famous throughout our family for being the focal point of the Maher clan, an end-of-terrace council house, bigger than it looked from the outside. It had three bedrooms, one bath, one indoor toilet and one outdoor toilet. There was a brick shed and a coal shed out back. We had a television with a meter on the side that you had to put a 10p coin in. I learned to pick a lock at a very early age and could open the coin tray so we could reuse the money. The remote control used to be on a lead that you plugged in to the front of the set.

In my early years there was no central heating and warmth came from a coal fire in the living room. We had paraffin heaters to heat the other rooms, there was no double glazing and the windows would ice up on the inside but it was homely and carpeted intermittently. The living room had what would now be very expensive parquet flooring but was carpeted most of the time.

We had two Jack Russells, Jonjo and Joe Joe, named after racing trainers and Dad built an aviary in the back garden for his canaries. He once trapped a few of the goldfinches in the garden and put them in the aviary with the canaries to try and get them to cross-breed. They did but the offspring ended up looking like thrushes – just brown and speckled. Dad also did a bit of gardening but we used to call it Irish gardening because there was no plan to it. Plants, vegetables and fruit bushes were all thrown together haphazardly.

There was always a lot of humour in the house. One of the running jokes in the family was that Mum was trying to kill Dad. We had a big glass cabinet which Mum used to keep her ornaments and glasses on display. She also had a habit of storing her sewing pins in random containers and there was one day when Dad came in from the pub and picked up an opaque glass from the cabinet to pour a drink in. Without looking he poured a whiskey, knocked it back and got a mouthful of drawing pins. Mum laughed her head off while he spluttered. It was all good natured. Another time I was in the kitchen when Mum came in laughing away to herself. She always did Dad a dinner tray and he'd sit in the front room and eat in front of the telly. I asked what the matter was and she explained that she'd left a bottle of penicillin one of the other children was taking on his tray and, without realising, he'd smothered it over his steak like ketchup and eaten it. He was as sick as a dog the next day. That was the sort of thing that happened to him all the time. Mum used Dettol which went white when you mixed it with water and which she kept in a milk bottle – with hindsight, probably not the most sensible place. One day, almost inevitably, Dad came in and took a swig thinking it was milk. After that he insisted he had lost his sense of taste.

We saw ourselves as cockneys, rather than Irish. Dad spoke with a funny accent and we spoke like Mum, the bona fide East-Ender. She loved jellied eels and regularly took us to Tubby Isaac's, one of the East End's iconic pie-and-mash shops. Her mum lived in Bethnal Green and we would go there all the time. We called her Little Old Granny No-legs. She had legs but she was so small that as kids we thought she didn't. She lived in a little flat and there were gaps all along her street where houses had been bombed.

Mum and Dad wanted me to go to a Catholic school so I went to St Anthony's primary school in Hainault, which was run exclusively by nuns, except for the assistant head. Every Tuesday we'd get marched down the road to the church for mass and I would faint regularly because I was allergic to incense. They'd have to carry me out.

From St Anthony's I passed my 11-plus and there were only two Catholic grammar schools I could go to, one of which was St Bonaventure's, miles away in Forest Gate. My parents selected it because it was the best. It was run by Franciscan friars who wore brown habits tied up with rope. The school was a big, old, imposing Victorian building which looked like Dartmoor prison. I had to get three buses there every morning and walk a mile and I hated the 90-minute journey. I was knackered by the time I got to school and resented having to go. I gave it a go for the first year or so but started to rebel soon after and would be among the regulars lined up outside the headmaster's office waiting for the cane. This was delivered to the backside or the hand depending on the level of the crime and the mood of the head.

Around the time of my school rebellion I started knocking about with the local skinheads, the sub-culture of choice for many young people in my neighbourhood. There were different crews in different areas and I was with the Manor Park crew. Allegiances centred around football clubs and we followed West Ham United. It was in the late 1960s and the skinhead movement grew just after the mods and rockers, but while mods and rockers fought each other, skinheads fought everyone, even each other. The whole movement was based around anarchy and trouble-making. I got involved because it was something to do. It spread by word of mouth and, every Saturday, Manor Park would meet up, loiter, cause a nuisance and then go to a game. There would be around 100–150 of us and at some point a fight would always break out. After the football we'd find a party to crash or we'd go to Stratford and beat up a rival gang. It was all good clean fun.

Being a skinhead wasn't just about football, fighting and cropped hair. There was a uniform too. You needed Doctor Martens boots; the more laces-holes the better. I knew people who paid money to have extensions sewn on the tops of their boots so they could add more. You also needed Levi jeans and Ben Sherman shirts, usually lime-green gingham-check.

Everyone stank of Brut, even the girls, and no one bought any-thing. If you couldn't afford a Crombie coat or a sheepskin you pinched one from the market or from a dance.

My embrace of the skinhead movement coincided with the curtailment of my academic career. Instead of going to school, I caught the bus to the swimming baths in Barkingside and spent the days there in the cafe with my mates.

The truant officer caught up with me eventually, much to the dismay of my mum, and I was expelled. The only school that took in expelled kids was Kingswood secondary modern in Hainault so I went there for the last year of school, by which time I was a lost cause. I was bored and I didn't find any of the lessons challenging. I messed around instead and I got kicked out of school again at 15 after setting up a booby trap over the door of one of the classrooms. It was a big, wooden desk lid. It hit the teacher on the head when he walked in. That was the final straw. I was just a couple of weeks away from leaving at the time anyway and was looking forward to going out and getting a job where I could earn money. Work was easy to come by and I got my first job digging septic tanks. I earned £10 a day which was good money for a 15-year-old, it kept me in gingham shirts and Brut.

CHAPTER 2

EDDIE GET YOUR GUN

The skinhead gang became my second family and West Ham's ground by Upton Park tube station became my second home. Football was a place to go on a Saturday afternoon. In those days, it was cheap to get in and you didn't need to have a season ticket. You paid on the door or you climbed over the turnstile and bunked in.

Everyone got in fights: normally there were running battles with away fans or other crews from other teams down Boleyn Road or Green Street. It was all quite organised. If a rival team such as Millwall or Tottenham was playing away, the supporters who didn't travel would catch a tube to Upton Park for a dust-up. Millwall fans hated everyone and everyone hated them. Notoriously, their club chant was, 'No one likes us, we don't care.'

Keeping such salubrious company, it was inevitable that sooner or later I would get in trouble with the law. But Manor Park weren't just football buddies, they were my mates too and we'd meet up as a group most nights and particularly at weekends, whether West Ham were playing at home or not. We had our regular hangouts, one of which was the midnight movies in Gants Hill. The films finished late and, rather than bother to go home, most of us would loiter, cause trouble and then go to the railway sidings by Ilford station nearby, kick a hole in the fence, climb through and go and sleep in the first-class carriages. It was cold but comfortable. The Crombie coats and sheepskins came in handy in the winter.

One night a bunch of us were running around after the movies, generally being loud and obnoxious, when I heard a smash nearby. One of the gang had put through the window in a jewellery shop on the high street and managed to bend the bars behind the glass wide enough to get a hand in. It turned into a free-for-all, a proper smash-and-grab. Everyone was reaching in and I joined the clamour and grabbed a string of pearls that I planned to give to my mum. The commotion and excitement roused a few people in the flats above the shops and lights started to go on. Everyone scattered in different directions and I legged it to an all-night snooker hall nearby along with a few others. On the way I put the pearls under a fence with the intention of getting them later. I assumed the cops would be along soon and I didn't want to get caught in possession of stolen goods.

A group of us bundled inside the snooker hall and, sure enough, after a couple of minutes, several police officers followed. They honed straight in on us. We were the only skinheads in the place and witnesses had seen us. I was grabbed roughly by an officer and dragged outside.

'I know it was you,' the copper growled. 'There are plenty of witnesses. Don't make things hard for yourself. Where are they?' He held out his hand for the goods.

'I don't know what you're talking about,' I said.

He slapped me around the head. 'There's a hard way and an easy way. Either way, you are getting nicked.'

I thought if I told him that I wasn't involved but that I knew where the pearls were, he'd let me off. I was 15 and stupid. I confessed and he dragged me out into the road and made me go and get the loot. I handed the necklace over to him and he quickly put it in his pocket. I wasn't surprised. I knew the law was bent and I knew they would end up sold to a dodgy fence somewhere. Cops were the biggest crooks around. The copper laughed and handcuffed me. I was thrown in a police van along with several of my unfortunate gang pals who had also been caught and we were driven to a police station where we were processed, slapped around, manhandled and then thrown in cells. I was a minor so my parents were called and an hour or so later the cell door opened.

'Maher, your mum's here to get you,' the custody sergeant sneered.

Mum had come to bail me out and was waiting outside. She had a face like thunder and was none too pleased. She was usually the one to dish out the bollockings at home. Dad kept out of it unless it was really serious, which this was and when I got home they both pitched in to tell me what a prat I was. I think they were also secretly more disappointed that I'd got caught than that I'd broken the law.

It turned out there was not enough evidence to charge me with theft so I was charged with receiving stolen property. I went to juvenile court and pleaded guilty. I was given a 24-hour attendance sentence – something like community service. I had to go to a centre once a week along with a bunch of other juvenile delinquents. It was always on a Saturday afternoon at 3pm, so we couldn't go to football. We sat around and did handiwork. I got quite adept at making baskets.

That was my first brush with the law and, if I'm honest, it was quite painless. It reinforced my general view that the police were not that bright. A few months later, another incident went even further to lower my opinion of the boys in blue. I was out one night with a mate called Keith and my brother Mick. We were walking down Ilford High Road past the Ilford Palais, a dance hall as unglamorous as it sounds. Just as we passed the front door we heard a car skid to a halt behind us. We turned around in unison to witness a squad car stopped at the kerb in a cloud of burned rubber. A bunch of old bill jumped out and made straight for us. I looked around to see who they were after and one of them grabbed me and pulled me aside.

'What's going on?' I said, struggling.

'Someone matching your description has been seen on the roof of a jewellers,' said the copper holding me. I was in my skinhead uniform: everyone matched my description.

'Get off me, I don't know what you're talking about,' I said. I was overly cocky and pushed the copper because I knew I was in the right. In response, he put me in an arm-lock. I swore at him.

Mick had also been grabbed. He managed to wrestle free and hit the copper who had me. Keith was also fighting with an officer. Mick's punch had the desired effect. The officer on me let go and I turned around and hit him. We started scrapping and another cop appeared. It was like a wild west brawl. At one point I looked over and saw Keith on the ground with one cop kneeling on his back and another on his knees, so I ran over and hit the copper on his knees. It turned into a free-for-all and reinforcements arrived. One by one, Mick, Keith and me were subdued. There were too many of them and they eventually carted us off.

Once again I found myself slapped around and thrown in a cell. We all got charged with assaulting the police but pleaded self-defence. We had been walking down the street minding our own business and were set upon. The case went to trial at Snaresbrook Crown Court and we were assigned a barrister who cross-examined each of the police officers involved. The barrister was intentionally antagonistic and one of the officers – a red-faced bloke called Donnelly – played right into his hands and lost his temper.

'You appear to have quite a short fuse, officer Donnelly,'

said the barrister with raised eyebrows. 'Are you sure that's not what happened that night? Are you sure these gentlemen were not just minding their own business and you mistook them for others and went in with heavy hands?' He turned to look at us.

Donnelly got even more agitated and started arguing. The judge had to calm him down. The officers were repeatedly asked how they tried to stop us from running away. Each one confirmed that we didn't try to flee the scene.

'So they stood there fighting and didn't run?' asked the barrister. Very skilfully he made the case that we were three innocents who had been jumped by the police and were just defending ourselves, which was the truth. Justice prevailed and we were all found not guilty. Once again Her Majesty's finest had come up lacking and, rather than bringing shame on the family, the community were pleased for us because at the time, that's how we lived and how things were. The police were on one side and we were on the other.

My brushes with the law abated for a while after my 16th birthday as I had other things to deal with. I became a father and a husband for the first time. Nowadays it seems very young but it wasn't uncommon back then for teenagers to get married and have children, especially those from Catholic families.

I had been introduced to Sandra by a friend who was dating her twin sister. He thought we'd make a good couple. We went out together, got on well and she got pregnant. We got married. She was 17 and I was 16. In my religion, you had a child and got married, no question, but in any case I was over the moon. I didn't feel shotgunned, it was my choice. We had to get permission from our parents because of our ages and they gave us their blessings. Although Sandra and our son are parts of my story, out of respect for their privacy I will not dwell on the details of our lives together and, let's be honest, you don't want to hear about that, anyway, do you?

The highlights are these: initially we lived with my parents at 99 and we got married in a registry office – there was no party, just the two of us and the witnesses. Sandra was pregnant at the time but not heavily. We dressed up nice, that was pretty much it. Then we went to the pub across the road. My son, Terry, was born in 1972. I was there at the birth. I was working in a warehouse at the time as a forklift operator. They called me down to the hospital.

The midwife handed me Terry and said, 'What a lovely boy.'

I replied, 'His head is shaped like a rugby ball.'

I did my fair share as a father and we had Mum there too. Anything we didn't know or understand, she helped out. She loved having a baby around the house. After I got married I got an apprenticeship with the North Thames Gas Board as a gas-fitter. I was good but they only paid £10 a week and, as a result, Sandra and I had no money. I struggled just to get together the fare to work, which was how brush with the law no. 3 happened. I 'borrowed' a moped for a couple of days that I found parked up one morning. I was charged with taking and driving away. I pleaded guilty and was put on probation. It was my last chance, the magistrate told me.

But a few months later I blew it again and the fallout changed my life. It started one Saturday at Ilford station. There was a game on and, as usual, I'd met up with the rest of the Manor Park. At the station, tickets were issued and stamped with the date using a handheld franking machine. The ink on the tickets was poor quality and could be rubbed off, which left you with a blank, slightly smudged ticket. On the day in question someone had stupidly left a franking machine on a counter at the station. The ticket office was shut and there was no one around. Seeing an opportunity to save my mates a few pennies, I grabbed it along with a handful of used tickets from the box where passengers threw away their used tickets and hurriedly walked off down the road, followed by a gang of mates.

I rubbed the dates off the used tickets, stamped a new date and passed a few out. I felt like Robin Hood walking down Ilford High Road with my band of merry skinheads, eager to share the spoils. But the one thing about a band of skinheads was that they always attracted attention. You didn't have to be a genius to work out that a crew of excited skins usually indicated some kind of petty crime. And so it wasn't a surprise when I felt my arm being tugged by the local constabulary who had been watching my antics and followed me down the street.

'What you got there, sonny?' the officer asked, eyeing the stamping machine in my hand.

'I found it,' I replied.

My mates, who had been loudly enjoying the fruits of my fortune a few seconds before, went uncharacteristically silent as the copper took the machine from me.

'I think you mean you stole it,' he said.

'I didn't. I found it in the street,' I said.

'You're nicked!'

And so, once again, I found myself back in the nick, arguing my innocence. This time I knew I was in trouble because I was still on probation for the moped theft. I was looking at a prison sentence. The Crown Prosecution Service realised they couldn't do me for theft because they couldn't prove where I'd found the machine but this just made matters worse, as they instead charged me with forgery, which carried a heavier sentence.

I was in a sticky situation and I resolved to turn myself around. I needed a plan. I didn't have much faith that I'd be lucky in the courtroom again. And then it hit me. I know, I'll run away and join the army, I thought. I discussed my plan with Sandra and explained that the law would probably not come looking for me in the army and, even if they did, a judge and jury would look favourably on me if I was a serving soldier. We'd also be eligible for married quarters, an added bonus.

Avoiding jail was not the sole reason I enlisted. I had been thinking about it on and off for some time, but the prospect of a prison sentence hanging over me was the nudge I needed. I went to the local recruitment centre and signed up to join the Royal Green Jackets, the regiment Paddy was in. I was accepted and hoped the long arm of the law wouldn't stretch as far as Winchester, which was where the basic training took place. Unfortunately, however, it did and before training I was required to declare any convictions or outstanding criminal investigations. I owned up and the army was not impressed. However, they were used to dealing with toe-rags in trouble and, rather than kick me out, they let me go to court and sent an officer along with me to vouch for me. The judge took kindly to the fact that I was trying to sort myself out and gave me probation again – with the proviso that the army became my probationer. It was fine with me.

The regiment was based in Catterick in North Yorkshire but I spent the first 16 weeks living in barracks in Winchester where I discovered I had a natural aptitude for marksmanship. I liked guns. I liked the feel of them and the technical and mental challenge of firing them accurately at a target. The first gun I fired was a self-loading rifle (SLR). It became apparent early on that I was a good shot. It just felt natural and I had good hand – eye coordination. I could judge distances well and quickly familiarised myself with a range of weaponry. I was also handy with the general-purpose machine gun (GPMG) and I qualified as a marksman, which was as high as you could get on both the SLR and the GPMG.

I was also first-class with a Browning 9 mm handgun and with a submachine gun. I had my shooting badges before I came out of training and was issued with an Enfield sniper rifle with a scope. I was pretty pleased with it at first, before I realised that on active duty it stood out from other weapons and made the owner more of a target. With the Enfield I could guarantee a hit from 800 yards and my performance on the ranges meant that, straight after training, I was selected to represent the British Army in a big international shooting competition in

Cyprus. I was flown out there for several weeks to continue my marksman training. Sandra and Terry continued to live at 99 and, when I returned from the Med, I was posted to Catterick where, after a while, I qualified for a married quarter and they came to live with me.

I spent more time shooting than anything else because I enjoyed it and I also realised that it was a good way of getting out of some of the more laborious tasks soldiers were called on to perform, such as litter-picking and drill. I joined the boxing team for the same reason although, while I was good at shooting, my prowess in the ring left much to be desired and I didn't take the training regime as seriously as some of the other more competitive pugilists. But all the same, training sessions took precedent over menial work. Soon I had a nice timetable worked out that allowed me to avoid many of the inconvenient day-to-day chores. Cleaning duty? Sorry, I've got target practice. Fag-butt tidy-up? Sorry, boxing training.

I enjoyed life in the army and to a degree it did calm me down and gave my life some direction. They say that the army sorts people out and teaches respect and values. It did, but I was still an idiot at times.

Drinking played a big part in squaddie life and we would regularly go out, get paralytic and get in fights with the military police (MP). It was just like being in another gang. Everyone hated the MPs, they were like the Millwall of the military, so on occasion we would go out and turn their jeeps upside down.

When I enlisted, I was told by some of the more senior soldiers in my unit that it was important to get my blood group tattooed on me in case I ever got injured in combat. After a few months at Catterick I took the advice and had the phrase 'B-positive' inked on my arm. It looked silly on its own so I had a rose-and-dagger design tattooed above it. It looked like one of those motivational pictures people pin on their fridges.

One night I got really drunk and some of my fellow soldiers took me into the local tattoo parlour and thought it would be funny to get the tattooist to draw a navy design on my arm. I woke the next morning with a stinking hangover and a navy tall ship on my arm above the words, 'Homeward bound to London town'.

About three months after training I was sent on my first tour to Northern Ireland. At the time the country was in the grip of the Troubles. British soldiers were sent in to keep the Catholic nationalists and the Protestant unionists from killing each other and became targets themselves. The country was riven with divisions, particularly in the capital, Belfast, which was where my unit was sent. I'd be lying if I said I wasn't apprehensive. We were stationed in the Whiterock, Westrock, Upper Falls area of Belfast. At the time it was rough and tense. The army shipped us over on transporters. There was a whole company on the boats and we got off in Belfast in the middle of what was ostensibly a civil war. We sat around on the docks with all our equipment waiting for transport to come and get us and take us to barracks. There wasn't a round of ammo between us. I remember thinking, If anyone does decide to attack, we'll be defenceless.

It was a dangerous place. Soldiers were regularly shot,

mortars were regularly fired and even the kids threw stones at us. We were not popular even though our role was to maintain peace and law and order. There were no effective police. The Royal Ulster Constabulary weren't equipped or trained for the scale of the problem so we filled the vacuum and did our best to stop the opposing sides killing each other and the whole area sliding into anarchy.

We were stationed in our own barracks and were there for four months. The barracks were surrounded by corrugated iron walls with sangars – towers manned by guards – at each corner. It was right in the middle of a residential area that looked like a normal council estate. There was a cemetery opposite the front gates and down to the left was the notorious Falls Road. The area was full of social divisions. You could drive down a road in a Catholic area and then suddenly would be in an area with British flags, controlled by Unionists.

Throughout the posting there were no days off, which was fine by me because the Falls Road wasn't the sort of place a British soldier would want to go for a friendly drink. No one went out and mixed with the locals, even though the Protestants loved us and saw us as their defenders – which we weren't. The tour involved a week of patrols, a week of sangar duty and then a week of stand-by that involved sitting around waiting to be called to action. We drove around in armoured vehicles, affectionately nicknamed Pigs, that people regularly threw rocks at. I was in the army for two years and did two tours that were thankfully uneventful for me, although I knew several people who were not so lucky and were shot during the Troubles.

One of the most nerve-wracking duties was snatch squad. There were regular demos against the army which usually descended into riots. Troublemakers used the demos to launch attacks against the soldiers trying to contain them. They would hide in the crowds, armed with rocks, firebombs and guns. The demonstrators were very organised. Women were placed in the front, then children, then the men. Shooters and petrol bombers would be behind everyone. The crowd would part for them and then close in afterwards. Snatch squads were tasked with going in to grab them. Normally we would patrol in flak jackets but in a snatch squad we stripped down to light clothing so you were faster and more mobile. There were four to a squad and we each had a cosh. The riot was in front of and we sat behind the riot troops. Squads were built for speed. We came out from the sides of the riot troops and ran behind the protestors to grab the main instigators and nick them. It was tense and the knowledge that there could be someone waiting for me with a loaded handgun in the crowd tended to focus my mind.

I had every intention of staying in the army and making it my future. It didn't work out that way, though. The government cut back numbers. When I got back from my second posting the company was going to Gibraltar. This would be a family posting for another two years but Gibraltar is small and they didn't have enough married quarters for everybody. Instead, I was told my services were no longer required. I was last in and first out. I got an honourable discharge. I was disappointed at the time but it turned out for the best because after a while I got my dream job and settled in to a life of law-abiding lifesaving.

CHAPTER 3

LONDON'S BURNING

If you did more than ten days' active service in the armed forces you got a General Service Medal and I wore mine with pride, even though my two tours of duty were mainly defined by boredom. I'd served Queen and country and represented the UK as a marksman. Not bad for someone who, several years later, became Britain's most wanted criminal. How the mighty fall, eh?

My exit from the army had been disappointing but when I left I was intent on staying out of trouble and continuing down the straight and narrow. I knew I had had a lucky escape two years previously. My probation was over but I couldn't afford to get into any more scrapes so I knuckled down and did a series of jobs to make ends meet. I didn't have any definite plans or a career path. I was interested in joining the fire brigade and filled in an application form but was informed that there was a long waiting list so I didn't hold out much hope. In the meantime, I turned my hand to anything. I was a trainee panel-beater and sprayer, I learned plumbing, I was a cutter in a butcher's shop (I hated that, it was bloody cold). Each job lasted a few months at a time because none of them particularly excited me. Unemployment wasn't an option because my parents had always instilled a strong work ethic in me and I wasn't one to laze around or claim the dole.

I managed to keep myself away from trouble for quite a while but taking opportunities was in my blood and I had a run-in with the law again after a silly incident in which I pinched some money from a milkman. I got a suspended sentence for that and then I kept my nose clean for several years. But trouble eventually found me again.

It's not as if I woke every morning and thought to myself, Right, what mischief can I get up to today? What law can I bend? I tried to be an upstanding, useful member of society. I really did. But trouble just seemed to follow me. I don't know what it was about me. Maybe it was the way I looked or the way I spoke.

It began when I found a job I liked, working in markets on the south coast. I was working on fruit and veg and women's fashion stalls in Winton, just outside Bournemouth and in Christchurch. I loved it down there. It made a nice change from the suburbs of east London and eventually my family moved there and I stayed for several years, settling down to work for a sheepskin and leather coat seller.

The market traders I worked with were all characters and, like me, were mainly from the East End. Most Fridays we'd meet up in the pub opposite the market for a few beers after work. On one afternoon one of the locals decided to take exception to the fact that there were a bunch of Londoners in his boozer. He got abusive and things got physical. The situation ended in a fist-fight during which I lashed out in self-defence. But I had a glass in my hand that unfortunately almost severed his ear.

Eventually the case went all the way to the Old Bailey because I pleaded not guilty. The trial date was set and I dressed up for court in a smart suit and tie. The other guy turned up in jeans and a cap-sleeved T-shirt that showed the tattoos all up his arm. He looked a right hooligan. I pleaded self-defence and explained that I had been minding my own business when he started on me. He hit me first, I hit him back, I didn't realise I had a glass in my hand. The case didn't last long. There was very little to argue about; it was my version against his. He claimed that I attacked him. The jury went out and when they came back in one of the panel gave me the thumbs-up. They had seen through the victim's sob story. Justice prevailed and I was found not guilty. I was dismissed and I walked out of court a free man and, once again, vowed to get on with my life like a good citizen.

In November 1979, after a brief stint as a financial advisor, I got a bit of good news. I had completely forgotten about my fire brigade application and now a letter arrived out of the blue inviting me to go along to a test and an interview at the London Fire Brigade headquarters in Lambeth. I was 24 and I had an eight-year-old son, so the chance of stability, a career with prospects and a pension couldn't have come at a better time. The country was in a terrible financial state. Margaret Thatcher and the Conservatives had come to power in May of that year and inherited an economy in tatters from the previous Labour government of James Callaghan. The nation was entering a long, hard recession. Inflation was in double digits. Unemployment rates were growing and about to get much worse. A safe, public-sector job was gold dust and I went to the selection day filled with hope. Along with other prospective employees I underwent fitness tests and was quizzed on my general knowledge. This included a rudimentary science test and an arithmetic test. I passed and got accepted, which was a big deal.

By then I was living in a council place in Wanstead and training took place at locations around London, depending on what I was learning. I was taken on as part of an expansion drive so there were lots of other new firemen training with me. Most of the training was done at Shoreditch station. It was bloody hard – in many respects, tougher than the army had been. There is a lot more to being a fireman than you would imagine. You have to know about fires and how they behave, you have to learn about building construction, materials, first-aid, physics, science, mechanics and engineering. It was like going back to school and doing army physical education at the same time. It was a skilful job and not something I could walk into without a high degree of preparation.

I went on residential courses at the fire service college in Moreton-in-Marsh in Gloucestershire, the biggest establishment of its type in the world. They had everything there: mock-ups of ships, car wrecks, dummy buildings they could set fire to or fill with smoke. Over the years I completed several courses and became a trained breathing-apparatus instructor, a trained first-aid instructor and I passed courses in rescues from crashed aircraft at sea, ship fires and became an emergency rescue tender operator. I did loads of different courses. I enjoyed it. It was the most rewarding career I had. Contrary to popular belief I do like helping people – as well as robbing them – and, although it's hard to believe, if you ever find yourself stranded at sea in the fuselage of a burning, crashed aircraft, you could do worse than be with me.

After I passed training I was stationed in Silvertown, an industrial district in the east of the city full of factories and warehouses. Much of the industry was in decline at the time. The area was rundown and ripe for development but the skyscrapers of Canary Wharf and Docklands hadn't been built and City airport was just a concept. Instead, the area was poor. It had the reputation of having the biggest fires because of the factories. The Tate & Lyle sugar refinery was on the patch and industrial fires were our bread and butter. On one shout we were called to a large piece of wasteland in the Isle of Dogs after a member of the public had reported explosions and fire. We raced to the scene and were confronted by several burning palm trees, bamboo huts and US army jeeps. We started putting out the fires and several men ran over from a Portakabin nearby and asked us to stop. It was a film set and they were filming *Full Metal Jacket*. The corner of Docklands we were standing on was supposed to be war-torn Vietnam. We stayed around for the rest of the day and watched the filming. After each explosion, we put the fires out so the film crew could reuse the props.

When we weren't on calls we continued doing training drills and maintenance on the equipment. One of the exercises that terrified me was the hook-ladder climb. The fire stations always had a tower at the back of them on which crews could practise. Hook ladders were ten feet long with big hooks on the end that could be secured over window sills. The aim of the hook-ladder climb was for me to start at the bottom of the tower and use my ladder to climb up the outside, floor by floor. From the ground I climbed to a first floor window, sat on the sill and carefully lifted the ladder up to the window on the next floor where I hooked it securely over the sill. Then I swung out onto the lower rung and climbed. I repeated the technique until I got to the very top of the tower and then went down the opposite side. It was terrifying but then there was a lot about being a fireman that was scary. It began with the first house fire I attended.

The shout came through and the alarm rang in the station. The training kicked in and I grabbed the woollen tunic (sounds impractical but it was the best fire-retardant material available) and headed to the engine with the rest of the guys on the watch. We knew it was a house fire before we got there and when we pulled up the building was well ablaze. The watch commander briefed us. They didn't know whether the house was empty or whether there were people inside and we needed to do a full sweep to find out. I pulled on my oxygen tank – breathing apparatus (BA) – and the full face-mask. We were sent inside in pairs.

Every fire is different. I very rarely saw anything inside a building except flame and smoke and no matter how much training I did, nothing could have prepared me for the first 'live' fire I walked into. As I was wearing a BA I had a limited field of vision. Much of the search was done through touch and I carefully made my way along the hall, feeling my progress and keeping within sight of the person in front. People react strangely in fires and will do anything to save themselves and their kids. They will put children in drawers or hide in random parts of the house, climbing into lofts or under beds so we were trained to search everywhere. The smoke was incredibly disorientating. Even people in homes they have lived in for decades get lost in fires. They can't find their way out of their own living rooms and curl up in a corner a few feet from the door to die.

Training taught me how to go into a burning room. I couldn't just open the door and walk in because I'd get a face full of fire. I had to feel the door first with the back of a hand. There are certain times in a fire when I had to ventilate to let smoke out but if I were to smash a window or kick in a door at the wrong time I would have got 'flashover', a sudden ignition of hot gas. You can look at building construction and see how certain building designs and materials will react; for example, a brick wall will shatter if it is too hot.

On that first fire I followed the lead of the men in front and we edged through the building room by room, checking every corner. We dragged hoses through with us, damping down the inferno as we went. At one stage the ceiling of one of the rooms we were in caved in and we had to duck to avoid the burning floorboards and plaster. We cleared the building and, thankfully, there was no one in it. It was exhausting work and there were some real squeaky-bum-time moments. Excuse the pun but it was a baptism of fire. After the blaze was under control I stood at the front of the building and looked on in awe of the damage that had been done in just an hour. A shell remained. It would always be depressing to see people's places after fires. The smoke and flames destroy everything.

Weeks turned into months. Silvertown fire station and the men in it became a home from home. There were four watches. 'Red', 'white', 'blue' and 'green'. The hours were brilliant. Everyone loved them and the union fought to keep them for years. We did two days on from 9am until 6pm followed by two nights on from 6pm to 9am, then we had four days off. Because we did not work during the day on a night shift, technically we had six full days off although, after a night shift, we still needed at least half a day in bed to recover. Despite the free time, we still worked a 42-hour week but we always seemed to be off more than we worked. Most people in the brigade had other lines of work too and, after a while I started to look for casual work that would fit around my commitments.

For a while, I worked for a security firm in Ilford and, in a twist of fate, was given a run delivering money in a security van. It was a small company and I never knew the extent of the money I carried. It was just a casual job as far as I was concerned and I never had any compulsion to drive off into the sunset. I was a trustworthy driver with a good career and prospects.

Eventually, though, another opportunity arose that was more attractive and promised better pay. I invested in a mobile baked-potato stand and we got a pitch at Donnington Park motor-racing circuit through one of my brigade friends, Paul, whose brother ran the catering and merchandising franchise at the Leicestershire venue. Eventually several of us from the brigade invested and we ran the whole catering service at the venue. It became very profitable and fitted nicely around the day job. We worked there for years and particularly enjoyed the annual Monsters of Rock festival. I saw some of the biggest bands in the world, including Aerosmith, Iron Maiden and Metallica.

I was earning a decent wage and bought a house in Elm Park, further out in the suburbs and a bit more open and green. I was a social climber and, towards the end of the 1980s, I decided to do something that some of my colleagues in the brigade did. I joined the Freemasons. For those of you who don't know, the Freemasons is a much misunderstood, non-religious, non-political, fraternal and charitable organisation. I had to ask to join a lodge and then I got vetted. I needed three sponsors from the lodge and went through a process of secret initiation and membership. I learned certain phrases and had to swear different vows. Over the years, masons have been linked to all sorts of skulduggery. Part of the code of masonry is that we look after our fellow masons, apparently leading to all kinds of abuses. Masons draw their membership from all walks of life, including the police, the legal profession and politics.

Suffice to say, I knew lots of people at a Clerkenwell lodge. It was a club and a fraternity. There were different positions in the lodge and I worked my way through the ranks. I got to the level of master mason.

People were attracted it because of the secrecy. It has been around a hell of a long time so there's a lot of history attached to it. In hindsight, I suppose I should have given some masonic signs at my eventual sentencing. Although I never officially rescinded my membership, I would imagine I wouldn't be welcomed back, which is a shame. I was told many years later that my disappearance caused a few red faces. Some of the police who were members of the lodge wanted me disbarred when I went on the run but it was pointed out that until I was convicted I was innocent, so instead I was placed on the list of lodge members who are absent and don't pay dues, placed on hold until the circumstances of my situation could be properly determined.

I wasn't classed as a fully qualified fireman until I had done four years in the service, after which time I progressed through the ranks and took my leading fireman and sub-officer exams. I passed, became a sub-officer and went to Stratford, the HQ of the area and a busy station. There were a lot of road accidents, rubbish fires, house fires and chemical jobs. I saw some very nasty shit.

On one shout we were called to an electric sub-station after reports that some kids had climbed in. One of the poor bastards had touched a live wire and melted. He was literally running down a wall. It was a sight that only those with strong stomachs could take.

At one RTA (road traffic accident) a car had crashed at speed against a concrete abutment under a road bridge. The car had gone over on its side and the driver's head was caught between the car and the wall. The speed of the impact had literally rubbed his head off. It was smeared across the wall while his headless body still sat slumped in the wreckage. At the time of his violent demise, he'd been eating fish and chips that were scattered over the road and still hot and steaming when we got there. One of my colleagues picked them up and ate them. Over time you hardened up. You had to. It was a defence mechanism, otherwise you'd go mad.

There was no shortage of drama at Stratford and when, on the night of 18 November 1987, I sat in the station on duty listening to details about a fire at King's Cross underground station unfold, I knew my watch would eventually be called to provide relief there. It soon became apparent that the brigade was dealing with a major incident. The fire was sucking in crews from around London and there were reports of multiple fatalities. Fire control let us know in advance that it was a big one and we started to prepare ourselves mentally for what we all knew would be a gruelling shift. Anxiety and excitement built.

The nearest stations were the first ones to attend and we listened over the radio as they got called out. The fire had first been reported by passengers at 7.30pm. It started in rubbish which had collected under a Piccadilly line escalator. Four fire engines and a turntable ladder were sent to the station and, at around 7.40pm, the decision was taken to evacuate. Several firemen went down to the escalator to assess the situation. They saw a fire about the size of a large cardboard box and planned to fight it with a water jet, using men with breathing apparatus. But within a few minutes the entire escalator was alight – that's how fast a blaze can spread – producing superheated gas that rose to the top of the shaft enclosing the escalator. The gas was trapped against a ceiling that was covered in many layers of old paint. The heat built up intensely until it ignited, causing a flashover that sent a jet of superheated flame and smoke into the ticket hall. The people caught in its path had no chance. With the upper level an inferno, several hundred people were trapped below ground.

Along with my colleagues, I sat in the station listening to all this, waiting to get the call. After about four hours we were told to go and relieve some of the crews who had been there from the start. We rushed to a scene that was organised chaos. You couldn't see anything from the ground except the smoke billowing out of the underground entrance, illuminated by the blue lights of the engines, ambulances and police vehicles parked on in every available space. A fire control unit had been set up and the progress of the crews beneath the ground was being monitored on a board that listed which crews were doing which duties.

The commander in control explained the details and the layout of the station. There were schematics of the tunnels spread out on a table. Our watch was tasked with rescue duties – essentially we were heading off for a subterranean search-and-rescue in a man-made cave system. With adrenaline surging, I got into my breathing apparatus and followed my colleagues into the main entrance and ticket hall, which was still alight in places. Scores of crews were inside, directing hoses at the walls and ceiling to damp down the fires. We picked our way through to the stairs and went down, blind, into the smoke-filled hellhole.

The heat was unbelievable. Firemen were passing out. There was fire, smoke and debris everywhere. We stayed in teams and followed hose-lines down into the bowels of the station. I focused intently on the person in front because the worst thing I could do in that situation was get separated. There were still lights on but the smoke remained impenetrable. It was like going into an oven and I was dehydrated in a couple of seconds. The sweat was streaming down my face inside my mask, stinging my eyes. The training got me through and stopped me panicking but every sinew in me was telling me to get out. There were no radios so we communicated by touch and if I got close enough to someone I could shout through my mask.

All the time as I made my way through the station I saw

people getting taken out. They were dazed, terrified and black with soot. The brigade rescued a lot of people from trains that had still been allowed through even as the fire was raging.

I was there for five hours in total, searching through tunnels, surfacing for a break and going back down again. It was physically and psychologically exhausting. I saw people with terrible burns and sometimes it felt like the job would never end, like the whole of London was burning. Yet by the early hours of the next morning the fire was under control but everyone was in a little bit of shock. Thirty fire crews – over 150 firefighters – were eventually deployed and 31 people died and 100 people were taken to hospital, 19 with serious injuries. The station officer in charge of the first pump to arrive, Colin Townsley, was in the ticket hall at the time of the flashover. He did not survive: his body was found beside that of the badly burned passenger he was trying to save.

The brigade was a close-knit unit of heroes. Fallen colleagues were honoured and remembered and I made some very good friends in the 11 years I spent as a fireman, such as Gary Thompson and Paul Collins. We depended on each other at times and it was inevitable that in the close confines of life-and-death situations we formed close bonds. There were around a dozen people on each watch and we all spent a lot of time with each other.

As well as the drama, there was also a lot of joking, messing around and black humour to get us through the nasty bits. In the dead of winter one time, when it was really cold, we attended a school fire. It was a large job and we were there for a certain number of hours until a relief crew came along. For a laugh, before we were called off, we threaded the hoses through the railings outside the school and filled them with water. It was the relief crew's job to recover the equipment and when they arrived the water had frozen solid in the hoses, making it impossible to remove them. There was always joking between watches and inevitably we'd leave booby traps and unpleasant surprises for the next watch after us to clear up.

I enjoyed the work and enjoyed the camaraderie. It was my career. I thought I had found my niche in life. It had been hard to get recruited in the first place and getting through training was an achievement. I worked hard at it and I got promoted a couple of times. During my time in the fire service I never got in any trouble. My convictions were spent and my life was stable. I wasn't one for going out and I mainly socialised with my colleagues. I remember one day I was at a family do and Mary, my elder sister, was there. I hadn't seen her for ages. Mick and my other brothers had been up to their usual shenanigans, getting in scrapes and Mary said to me: 'You're the boring one now.'

I laughed. 'Yeah, I'm just a fireman,' I replied.

CHAPTER 4

TIME, GENTLEMEN, PLEASE

Mary had said I was boring but, of course, she meant in relation to the characters that we grew up with who, even in adulthood, were still all at it in one way or another. It was all petty stuff; knock-off gear here, dodgy car sales there.

There were rules. They never took from people like us and they looked out for our own. If one of us was going to take something, we took it from people who could afford to lose it. No one had any sympathy for the big businesses – the banks, building societies, insurance companies and faceless organisations that ripped people off. They were legitimate targets. As long as no one got hurt, it was OK to have one over on them. Even the police turned a blind eye to the low-level antics that were common around London in the 1980s. It was the same in the fire brigade – everyone ducked and dived to a degree. There were a few shady little businesses and cash-in-hand jobs that were never declared. One of the popular money-making schemes was the naughty video market. In the days before the internet, blue movies came on VHS cassette and were tightly controlled by government regulations. You could only buy them in licensed shops and they cost a fortune . . . apparently! So, all over the country, enterprising individuals rented them out or linked up several video machines together and made pirate copies. Many found their way to the London fire brigade and were circulated throughout the service, rented out for a pound a night. It was nice little sideline for the blokes who ran it and I doubt they ever declared it on their tax returns.

Despite the little schemes many of us had going, we were all honest when it came to our jobs. We had access to people's homes and businesses after all and no one I knew ever took advantage of that or of the people we were helping. There were lines that just wouldn't be crossed and no firemen I knew would ever think for a minute of betraying the trust between the public and the service. As firemen, we were all totally professional when it came to the job of fighting fires, saving lives and dealing with emergencies.

The service was also very serious about training. Everyone was expected to go on regular courses to keep up to date with the latest equipment and techniques. Most of the courses were held in Moreton-in-Marsh and, in 1988, I found myself there on an emergency rescue tender course. There were fitness sessions held daily and one turned into a rugby game. Before

I joined the brigade I had played football, but rugby was a popular game throughout the service and I got hooked on it and on golf, too, which most firemen played (it must have been something to do with all the time off).

Like most rugby matches played between firemen, the one in question was spirited and, when one of my colleagues made a run to attempt to score a try, I put my arm out to try and stop him. He ran straight through it. I heard the crack and felt an immediate searing pain in my shoulder. I looked down at my t-shirt and my arm was pointing in the wrong direction. It had dislocated and popped right out of the shoulder socket. Luckily, with my first-aid training I knew what to do and I grimaced as I popped the arm back into place with a sickening click. It was painful for a few days afterwards and was black all over but I expected the pain to subside. Over the following days however, it got worse. If I slept with it in the wrong position I lost all strength and feeling. It also took a few minutes to start functioning after I woke. If I was on night duty and asleep when a call came through, it took a while to get feeling back as I tried to dress myself and get to the engine. If I held my arm in certain positions it was painful. I carried on for weeks after the injury in the hope that it would improve but at the back of my mind I knew I'd done something serious to it and eventually I went to the GP and was referred to a specialist.

I had scans that revealed that I had damaged the sac and tendons around the joint. I had physio but it got worse and, slowly, the severity of what had happened dawned on me. It wasn't going to get better and I could no longer do the job I loved. When it was apparent that I couldn't work at the required level I was signed off on sick leave. I was sent for evaluation and the specialists used electrodes to test the sensitivity in my nerves. There was a threshold figure – if you could function with more than 70 per cent capacity in your arm, you could work. Below 70 per cent and they classified you as incapacitated and unfit for the job. After a year of tests and treatment while signed off sick, a medical tribunal finally declared me unfit to work and, to my huge disappointment, I was retired out of the service.

I was gutted. I had been in for 11 years and never thought I'd do anything else. Being a fireman is a way of life. It was my identity. It wasn't just a job, it was who I was. Suddenly my whole identity was compromised. I didn't know what I was going to do. I got a pension but it wasn't enough to live on. By the time I left I was a sub-officer with prospects. I had a tight social circle and a comfortable professional life. The money was good and, had I stayed, I would have been comfortable for the future. I had no debts and a decent house. I left the London fire brigade with a heavy heart, full of uncertainty.

My life was at a crossroads in other ways, too. Things had not been good in my marriage for several years. Sandra and I had drifted apart and, although I wasn't looking, I couldn't help but be drawn to an attractive, fun woman who caught my eye when I happened to be in the bar of a guest house near Donnington. I had continued to be involved in the catering business and regularly made trips to the Leicestershire race circuit. After I was pensioned out of the brigade, the business provided a lifeline and I enjoyed the opportunity to get away and earn some money. As the years had gone by we had expanded from our initial baked-potato stall and, in the end, we more or less owned the whole catering concession for the park. We used to sell the concessions off to other caterers and also continued with the spud business. We split it four ways so none of us were ever going to be millionaires but it was a nice little earner and it allowed us access to concerts and events.

When we were there we stayed in the same guest house and we knew the owners, Ray and Louise, very well. After working a night at the venue we would get back late and, much to Ray's annoyance, help ourselves to drinks in the bar – which we always paid for – and then raid the kitchen and eat the bacon Ray had cooked and set aside for breakfast the following morning. One night, around the time I was still officially a fireman but waiting for the brigade to decide my fate, there was a group of women in the bar and we got chatting. One in particular caught my attention.

Debbie Brett was tall, beautiful, confident and funny. I don't know what she saw in me, I'd had a few drinks and was acting a bit of an idiot, but we clicked and spent several hours laughing and joking. Debbie was an air hostess and was training nearby. I wasn't looking for anyone and I wasn't out to hurt Sandra but I felt like I'd known Debbie all my life and I asked for her number. After that night we met up again and I knew that she the one for me. My marriage crumbled further, I got divorced. It wasn't friendly. Debbie supported me and stuck by me and when she was transferred to Gatwick airport we got a place together in Crawley first and eventually in Dartford. I was in the process of leaving the brigade when it all happened and it was a stressful year but moving in with Debbie made it all seem right. She was the one positive thing while everything else seemed to be going wrong.

As the dust settled we began to discuss our future. Terry was in his mid-teens at the time and lived with his mum but came and stayed with us when he wanted to. I did a few different jobs and concentrated on the catering and the months rolled by. It was an uncertain time and in the middle of it all, to complicate matters even further, Debbie announced that she was pregnant. I like to think that I can take things in my stride and, although we hadn't planned to have a baby, I knew what the results could be when I put certain things in certain places and so it didn't come as a complete shock. The baby was unplanned but not unwanted and we were both pleased, if not a little apprehensive. Debbie gave birth to our son, Lee, and we settled in to domestic life while I worked out what to do for our future.

By that time I had a small lump sum from the brigade and I started to consider investing some of it. When my brother Paddy had retired from the army several years previously he had become a landlord and he seemed to enjoy the life. It provided a roof over his head and a wage, so Debbie and I looked at that as a future together and found a pub in a village called Higham in Kent, near Rochester. The pub had been shut for a while and was owned by a brewery called Shepherd Neame. We went to view the place – the Gardeners Arms – and drove into Higham full of optimism for the future. It was a small village with one main road.

The Gardeners Arms had two bars and a beer garden, it smelled damp and the kitchen needed refitting. It was nondescript but the pub at the other end of the street was successful so we figured there would be enough business to go around. I spoke with the brewery rep and had to go to court to get a landlord's licence. I didn't have to declare my previous convictions because they were spent and I hadn't been in trouble for many years. I was a former fireman and ex-serviceman, exactly the sort of upstanding citizen the brewery wanted running their pub. My name went over the door and in 1991 we opened for business.

It didn't take long to realise what a nightmare lifestyle owning and running a pub was. We had a young toddler to look after and the hours were gruelling. To begin with, we did OK and we broke even. There was enough regular trade to keep the tills ringing. I played along in the role of landlord. I had a Daimler Sovereign parked out back (a fitting landlord's motor) and when that went wrong, rather than pay for new parts, I bought an old breaker and parked that out back too. We tried to be part of the community and make friends. Every Sunday lunch, Debbie cooked roast potatoes and put them out on the bar as a freebie to entice punters. We covered them in salt to make people thirsty, in the hope they'd buy more beer, an old trick that worked.

Day by day, week by week we kept the thirsty folk of Kent supplied with bitter, lager, spirits and wine. It was hard slog with long days and between it all we had to juggle looking after Lee. We didn't have a manager and it was a seven-day-a-week operation for tick-over money. Everyone assumed I was rolling in it, mainly because of the two cars. It couldn't have been further from the truth. My payout from the fire service had gone because I sunk a lot of extra money in renovations to the pub. I was struggling to stay afloat.

Then we started having trouble with a couple of the local hard cases after we barred one of their cousins for exposing himself to one of the barmaids – classy eh? The family were well known in the village. The landlord from the pub down the road had warned us about them but I didn't care what reputation they had – I wasn't going to let that sort of behaviour go unnoticed. These brothers came in and started shouting the odds, telling me they were in charge and insisting I let their pervert cousin back in. I stood my ground and told them where to go. They swaggered off, threatening retribution and, sure enough, that night a concrete block ended up in the back window of one of my cars. Luckily the idiots targeted the breaker and not the roadworthy one. At that point I should have gone to the police but it wasn't in my DNA. I had no proof anyway. And as a new landlord the last thing I needed was police attention. My livelihood depended on being a licence holder and if the licensing authority – the local council – deemed me incapable of running the place effectively they could strip me of my licence and put me out of work.

I hoped that was the last of it and I heard or saw nothing for the next few months. We carried on with pub life and continued to make a go of things. Then one night Debbie was away with Lee at her mum's and I was in the pub with Terry who was staying for a few days. In the early hours I woke up to the sound of breaking glass and lay in bed for a few seconds trying to work out what was going on. As soon as I smelled smoke I jumped up – my fireman's instincts were still sharp. I shouted to Terry who had also been woken by the noise of breaking glass. I pulled on a pair of trousers and we both ran out onto the landing. There were wisps of smoke rising up the staircase and I could see an orange glow coming from one of the bars downstairs. I went down quickly but carefully and told Terry to stay close behind. The fire was in the bar at the back of the pub and I could see it had already taken a hold. I could smell petrol fumes. It was obvious that we'd been petrol-bombed.

Thankfully there was a way out the front and Terry and I got out the building quickly. While he ran off to the nearby phone-box to call 999, I ventured around the side of the building to see if there was anything I could do. Years in the fire service had taught me how quickly a building fire can take hold and I knew there was nothing I could do when I saw the extent of the flames. I stood outside and listened to the sound of the spirit bottles exploding while I waited for the firemen to come.

They arrived in minutes and soon got the blaze under control. They managed to contain the damage to the back bar area but the smoke had spread through the whole building and ruined everything. Our furniture, our clothes – all our possessions reeked of smoke and most of them had to be thrown out.

There was no way we could open again until we completely refurbished and redecorated so the doors were locked up. In the days after the fire we salvaged what we could and moved out to a rented house for a while to let the insurance assessors and then the builders do their work, which took months, during which time I wasn't earning. We both wondered whether a pub really was the best place to raise a child and realised we would have to think about what we were going to do.

With work progressing on the pub we had another upheaval. Dad had been getting frailer. Initially, we assumed it was his age. Years of back-breaking work on building sites had taken their toll and, although he was a fit man, he had been slowing down. Several years before, mum had been diagnosed with pancreatic cancer and she had beaten it. Many people think pancreatic cancer is an automatic death sentence and it's true to say that it can be one of the most virulent forms of the disease but, thankfully, the doctors got Mum's before it spread and she had her pancreas removed, making her instantly diabetic but saving her life. The illness and shock had affected Dad and, faced with the prospect of losing the love of his life, he'd aged overnight. When he started complaining of stomach pains, tiredness and nausea we thought it was just his age, but the problems persisted and finally he went to the doctor who referred him for tests. In a tragic twist, he was diagnosed with the same cancer that Mum had beaten years before. The diagnosis knocked us all for six.

With so much going on in our family life and with our career in limbo while we were waiting for the grand reopening of the

Gardeners Arms, we decided to use the last of my savings and take a holiday. We both deserved it and we wanted to be fresh for the challenges that lay ahead. My brother Michael knew people in New Hampshire in the USA and had spent a lot of time over there. He always talked about what an amazing place it was. Debbie and I had never been to the States so we decided to book a fly-drive down the east coast and booked a flight into Canada. There we hired a motorhome with the intention of driving all the way down to Memphis. It would be an adventure and an experience for Lee.

We flew into Canada in the middle of one of the coldest winters the eastern seaboard had experienced. It was minus-20 and so cold that the tears in our eyes froze. We went to pick up the motorhome and were told not to use the shower in it until we got further south because the pipes would freeze. That year there was also record flooding so we never made it down to Memphis: the furthest south we got was Carolina and even there it snowed. For most residents, it was the first time they had seen snow.

We spent most of our time in New England and loved it. It was a different way of life to the drab slog that we were used to. It was leisure-orientated and people worked to live, they didn't live to work. One day, in passing, I mentioned to Debbie that I could quite happily live in a place like that. She agreed. It seemed like the ideal place for a young family.

We returned to the UK and Dad continued to deteriorate. The cancer was spreading and, despite his belief that he could beat it, he got weaker. Debbie, Lee and I moved back in to

99 to help Mum look after him. She wanted him to go into hospital because she couldn't stand to watch him get worse but we all knew he'd be happier at home. We knew that he was going to die and it broke our hearts. While he was still able to walk, Debbie, Mum and me took him back to Ireland and to Templemore, where his family had come from. It was a bittersweet homecoming. We all knew it was the last time he'd ever go there. He enjoyed Ireland; he showed us where he'd been born, below the Devil's Bit mountain – so-called because the devil was supposed to have taken a bite from it. A lot had changed in the country since Dad was there and much of it was unrecognisable. But we met some family who knew him and the Maher family name was all over local businesses.

The cancer showed no mercy and Dad went downhill quickly when we returned. I had to carry him to the bathroom when he lost strength. It was hard to see. Dad had always been so strong. We had ups and downs but we were close, he was still my dad and I loved him. No matter how you cut it, cancer robs you of dignity. In the last days Dad couldn't get up and had to have a commode. He was on loads of morphine to dull the pain and ease his exit from life. He slipped away when I was out of the house. I'd gone to get some medication and when I came back he was dead. Mum was there with him holding his hand. He always joked that she kept trying to kill him. In the end she couldn't let him go. She stayed with him for hours, holding on, hoping he'd come back to her. It was heartbreaking. He was her everything. All she knew was him. They'd been together for so long they'd grown into one. At the end he was comfortable and died at home in his castle – 99.

The funeral was a big affair, full of friends and family. After that, Mum was quiet for weeks. I was devastated. In life, always tell people that you love them because you never know when they might go. I wasn't there at the end but I'm so glad I had time with him. He was a big man was Jimmy Maher. He was one of a kind.

In hindsight his death probably made me re-evaluate my life. Debbie and I talked and we realised what a mistake we'd made with the pub. It was no life and it certainly wasn't a place where we wanted to bring up Lee. I wanted to spend time with my son because time goes very quickly. As soon as work on the pub finished, we put it back on the tenancy list. It didn't take too long before a couple came along who had run pubs before. We told them everything. We told them about the fire and the trouble and they were happy with it. They took over and we moved out.

We got a rental place in South Woodham Ferrers in Essex. We had no money but I felt free. Once again I started looking for work.

CHAPTER 5

IN THE 'COR

It was almost as easy to get a job with Securicor as it was to drive off with one of their vans. I was only out of work for a few weeks before I was handed the keys to a van loaded with money.

A lot has been made about my choice of career after the pub. According to newspapers and the police, I applied for the job with Securicor because my intention was always to steal money, even though I hadn't been convicted of any crime for over 20 years and had since served my country as a soldier and served the community as a fireman. It was true that in my youth I had stolen some jewellery, borrowed a moped, got in some fights, clumsily reprinted some rail tickets and pinched money from a milkman. This, according to the legend that grew around me, qualified me as a master criminal, intent on depriving 24 banks of their weekend cash delivery.

The truth is less dramatic. I applied for a position with Securicor when I saw it advertised. I needed a job, I wanted to work somewhere with flexible hours that would allow me to spend time with Debbie and Lee and I already had experience delivering cash in transit as I'd done it for a short while when I was in the fire brigade. Plus, I had a thing for uniforms, but that's our little secret!

I applied for the Securicor job in March 1992. I filled in the application form and I went for an interview. It was quite common for former members of both the military and the emergency services to end up in jobs that involved some form of security. I didn't fancy myself as a bouncer or a night watchman, so being a driver seemed a little more accommodating. It was never meant to be a career, just a stop-gap while I worked out my long-term options. On the application form, I was required to give details of previous convictions. In the UK, the Rehabilitation of Offenders Act says that after a certain period, convictions do not have to be declared. The idea of the rule is so people who commit silly, petty crimes when they are young and foolish do not get penalised repeatedly for them for the rest of their days. It allows people like me to take our punishment and get on with our lives, which I had done. I did not tell Securicor about my wayward youth because as far as I was concerned I wasn't required to.

I got the job and, by October, I was on a permanent contract. It suited me and it couldn't have come at a better time because

I was struggling to make ends meet. Debbie was at home looking after Lee and we had rent to find and all the usual outgoings of a young family. I had that small pension from the fire brigade but even with that I was living from pay cheque to pay cheque. The pub had sucked up my payout and I had borrowed some too. We were trying to help Mum out as well because she was struggling after Dad's death.

Securicor was the biggest cash carrier in the UK. In the early 1990s, it reportedly carried £100 billion a year using a fleet of 1,500 vehicles and enjoyed a 56 per cent market share of the cash-in-transit business. Set up in the 1930s, the company started out supplying night guards to watch over London properties. It diversified in the 1980s, went into partnership with British Telecom and pioneered a vehicle tracking system called Datatrak, which was fitted to most of its vans.

When I first started at Securicor they sent me on a residential training course for a couple of days, along with several other new drivers from all over the UK. Senior Securicor staff took us through the routines and explained the security measures and protocols that we were expected to follow. One of the more memorable elements of the training was being shown the company's anti-robbery measures, which consisted of a pickaxe handle with a metal tip on it. These were standard issue for all crews and to be used for protection and to foil raids on vans. When the bloke taking the course showed us the equipment, there were a few raised eyebrows in the room as people tried to work out what good a stick would be against a blagger with a sawn-off shotgun.

Mr Securicor explained, 'Attacks on vans are on the rise and one common method of attack is with a mechanical saw. The robbers will use cutting equipment to get inside the van. The poles can be used to strike the blade and break it as it comes through the van shell.'

'Break blade with stick,' I wrote on my pad, shaking my head.

The delivery protocols were explained. Because thefts and robberies were on the rise there were very strict processes designed to cut down risk. Guards could carry no more than £25,000 at a time outside a van. This often led to guards having to make two journeys per delivery so, although it lessened the amount that could be snatched, it effectively exposed the guard to twice the risk. But hey, at least the bosses reduced their own exposure. Anyone who carried more than £25,000 faced instant dismissal. Every delivery had to be made by a two-man team with one guard making the drop while the other waited in the van. Every delivery and collection had to be signed for.

During training we were also shown the layout of the trucks. Securicor owned several different makes and models but all the cash delivery vans had the same layout. They were bulletproof and armoured. There were no doors for the driver or passenger, just the airlock-style entrance at the side. This was big enough for a couple of people to get through and had two doors. The doors were fitted with a mechanism that meant they couldn't be opened at the same time and the outer door was fitted with a lock that was controlled by a switch in the driver's compartment. There was one key that fitted both the locks. To get out of the van a guard had to open the interior door with his key, get in the airlock, close and lock the interior door then open the exterior door. The key was left in and when the guard came back, the driver opened his door using the buzzer. The system was designed to ensure that an intruder could not get in or out of the van. The airlock also had an escape hatch, in case someone got stuck. The hatch was alarmed.

Before each delivery run, cash was loaded in the van at the depot. The cash was pre-bagged and tagged according to where it was being delivered so you never knew how much you were carrying. At the delivery location one guard would check the order, place it in the carry case then put the case in the chute that led to the outside. The inner part of the chute would be closed and the guard would go through the airlock to the outside where he could take the case from the chute and deliver the goods.

Every recruit began as a driver and then worked their way up to being allowed out to deliver the money, where they were most at risk. Rookies went out with someone more experienced to learn the ropes. In theory, staff were supposed to change delivery runs regularly but in practice people had their favourite jobs and runs and tried to stick to them. It made sense because you got to know an area and could do a familiar run quicker than a new one. Night jobs suited some people and initially I did the night shift filling up ATMs because the shift pattern meant I could spend the day at home helping Debbie with Lee. There were three of us on the ATM route. We had keys for the cash machines on the route and we filled little metal cassettes with notes at each location and slotted them into the machines, ensuring that there would be enough money in them for the morning rush hour.

After a few months on the job I stopped thinking of my cargo as money. There was so much of it all the time I became desensitised. We were like any delivery drivers and our vans were just delivery vans. With Yodel drivers, it is clothes, with Amazon, it's parcels, with Securicor it was cash. The money was kept covered anyway so I tended to forget about it. Staff didn't walk around wide-eyed and scheming how to pinch the cargo from the back of the vans. Instead they joked about it and several of them pinched a bit here and there. On the ATM routes I often heard of people helping themselves to a tenner here and a twenty there and people would talk about how you fiddle with the mechanism inside a cash machine to make it distribute £20s instead of £10s. Given the chance, most people will look for any way to make a bit on the side and security guards were no different.

The real riches were not in the vans anyway. They were in the depot or the vault, as it was called. It was on an industrial estate in Chelmsford and it was where all the money was stored before it was divided into deliveries. The firm had big, three-tonne armoured trucks that went on regular runs up to an even bigger Securicor distribution centre in Nine Elms in London. That was the main depot. Banks would order money that was taken there and distributed to the regional centres like the one I worked from. Nine Elms was huge. The money that went there came direct from the Bank of England. There were pallet-loads of cash in those types of places. In 2006 the main Securitas depot in London got done, a similar place. That time, £53m was taken – there was so much cash missing the Bank of England had to decide whether or not to issue new bank notes.

The big trucks from Securicor would go to Nine Elms once or twice a week, fill up and bring the money back to the vault where there were people counting it and putting it where it was supposed to go. I never worked in the vault but I drove through it regularly. From the vault you picked up your daily delivery. You would get a breakdown of the run you were doing that told you the seal numbers of the bags you were going to pick up. You would drive into the vault and load your delivery into the van. One of you would get in the back. Sometimes when you loaded you would make chairs out of the bags of money to sit on. They were inviting people to nick it, people were sitting on two million pounds in cash. After you loaded in the vault you'd drive out for the day, with your money chair swaying in the back.

Most of the people working at the depot were the same as me, middle-aged blokes trying to make a living. Many were former service personnel. There was nothing special about most of them and, although they were perfectly pleasant, I didn't make any particularly close friends. I wasn't there that long. They all joked about robbing and there were always stories about guards nicking money out of the back of the van. They were probably true. People nicked money, got caught and got fired but you never heard about it officially because it would make the company look bad and the company had to maintain an image of trustworthiness and integrity for the sake of its commercial success.

There were different crews on different routes and the routes were the same each day with the same drops. The only thing that changed was the amount delivered. After several weeks on the ATM route I got fed up of nights. As I got more experience I could apply for different routes and the one we all wanted was the bank route. That delivered to banks in Suffolk and Essex and it was attractive because it paid more and it finished earlier. Most people didn't care too much what route they were on but I wanted to get back home early so I applied. It was later made out that I angled to get on that route because I wanted to rob it but that was never the case. It was only after I got that route that things started to go pear-shaped. What I didn't realise was that being on the bank route made me a target.

CHAPTER 6

THE SET-UP

You know sometimes there's a knock at the door and you just know something unpleasant is waiting for you on the other side? It's like a sixth sense. Maybe whoever is doing the knocking is banging a little too hard or a little too insistently. Whatever it was, I knew that there was aggro waiting for me that night in January 1993.

Debbie and I were sitting on the sofa watching something on the TV. Lee, who was three, was asleep upstairs. It was late. I can't remember exactly what time but late enough to warrant a raised eyebrow and a 'Whoever can that be at this time?' There's a visiting watershed. After about 9pm, anyone who knocks at your door uninvited and unplanned is there for a reason.

I walked out of the living room and shuffled to the front door to open it. It was dark outside and in the gloom there were two men standing on the doorstep. My spider sense was tingling. Body language tells you a lot about someone and they say that first impressions count. Well I could tell by their subtle body language that the blokes outside were nasty bastards and my first impression was that I didn't like them.

'Hello?' I said.

'Eddie Maher?' one of them asked.

'Who's asking?' I replied.

The speaking one – Mr Chatty – answered with another question, ignoring me. 'Is Debbie and baby boy in?'

'Why?'

The quiet one had been standing in the shadows behind Mr Chatty. He stepped forward in what I assumed was an attempt to be menacing. The light from the hallway lit his face. The gods of good looks hadn't been kind to him. Picture a stereotypical thug. That was him. Tall, stocky, missing teeth, crooked nose, hooded brow, scars, shaved head, black eyes, tattoos on his neck. He looked like Vinnie Jones's ugly older brother. Mr Chatty, on the other hand, was slightly smarter. He wore a leather bomber jacket with a white polo shirt underneath. He was clean-shaven, younger and thinner. He spoke with a typical cockney accent and had unusually white teeth. Scarface sniffed and stared at me. Mr Chatty asked me again.

'Debbie and your boy, are they in? We need to have a word with you but it's best we keep it to ourselves. We wouldn't want to upset anyone.' Upset anyone? What did he mean? I was wrong-footed. It sounded suspiciously like a threat.

Debbie called from the lounge. 'Who is it Eddie?'

Mr Chatty nodded and smiled. His question was answered. 'We'll talk again Eddie. We'll come back tomorrow,' he said.

'What's this about?' I asked as the two of them turned and walked off down the drive.

'Nothing to worry about,' Mr Chatty replied. 'We just want a chat.'

As they walked away I noticed a car parked at the front of the house. I couldn't work out the make. There was someone driving. It was too dark to make out who it was. The two men got in and the motor drove off slowly. I went back inside. My heart was racing. I had unsettling feeling.

'Who was that?' Debbie asked when I sat back down.

'Don't know,' I answered. 'They were looking for the people who lived here before.'

Life was a grind. Day in, day out I was driving the van and trying desperately to make ends meet. I was never any good with money and never had been. As soon as I had it, I spent it. I never planned for the future. I struggled by with the blind faith that I would manage somehow and something would turn up. It usually did. Growing up where I had, when times were hard I always believed that – with a bit of ducking and diving and a bit of luck – I'd be able to make enough to get by. I wasn't a shirker. I had always worked. But in the early 1990s, when the country was in another recession, it was tough to keep up with the cost of living.

One of the many misconceptions that surfaced about me when I went AWOL was that I had built up loads of debts and that I amassed some gambling debts too. That's not the truth. Sure I had debts, I had overdrafts and some money owed on credit cards but no more than many people and certainly not enough to justify the course of action I took. I wasn't a big gambler either. I played cards sometimes and I was good at it. As a rule, I didn't lose money. The debts I had were as a result of living expenses, rent, food, a young child to keep and my failure to manage money effectively.

The reason I did what I did had less to do with debt and more to do with the strange men who turned up on my doorstep that night and returned the day after when Debbie was out. They seemed to know when I was on my own. I assume they had been watching the house. They arrived and invited themselves in. There were three of them this time. The driver had obviously parked up and accompanied them. He was a weaselly looking bloke – ratty – with a hooked nose and bulging eyes. I stood aside in the hallway and let them walk past. At this point, the more astute readers will be asking: 'Eddie, why did you just let them walk in?' Good question. Because I knew they were gangsters. That spider sense I mentioned earlier was tingling from the minute I clocked eyes on them. They certainly weren't there to read the meter. I grew up in the East End. I hung out with skinhead gangs. Dad worked the building sites. My manor was full of crooks. I could spot one a mile away. These blokes had an air about them. They say you know your own and while I wasn't the criminal element, I knew a criminal – or three – when I saw them.

Scarface was playing the part of bad cop again and pushed

past me. I have learned since that just because someone has got scars, it doesn't mean they are tough. If you want to find the tough one you find the bloke who gave him the scars. However, he looked like trouble and I stepped aside to let them in. They walked brazenly into the kitchen and I followed.

'Bit nippy, eh, Eddie?' Mr Chatty said.

'Cut the crap, what do you want?'

The thing is, I sort of knew what they were after.

It all started a couple of weeks before. I'd been in one of the locals I used to drink in over in Ilford – the sort of place frequented by the three geezers in my kitchen – and I'd been having a few pints with some old mates. We were talking. I'd had a few and my tongue was loosened. As was often the case when people realised what I was doing for work, the banter began: 'How much have you nicked?', 'Would anyone know if you helped yourself to a couple of grand?'

They were questions I'd been contemplating myself. Not because I planned to steal anything but because others in the depot joked about it too. It was a little game they played. How can you take money without it being noticed? I'd thought about it and I had a simple theory. 'Why would you mess around and risk getting caught for the sake of a few hundred? It's pointless. There's a simple of way of doing it. You take the van, not the money,' I explained. It wasn't rocket science. Why mess around pocketing a few notes here and there? Theft is theft, if you wanted to steal and risk prosecution, make it worth your while.

'But aren't the vans locked?' my mates questioned.

'It takes two people to work the system that allows you to get the money out,' I said. 'If there are two people in on it, you can get the money out of the van.'

It was not a sophisticated idea. There were no clever devices needed or expert knowledge. It was later suggested that I had trained as a locksmith to gain expert knowledge on picking locks. That was rubbish. True, I had briefly worked in a locksmith business but I didn't need any special skills to get the money out. Two people could fit in the airlock. The lock could be triggered and you could both get out. It suited the papers, the police and Securicor to paint me as a criminal mastermind after the theft to save their embarrassment. The truth of the matter is that the most notorious crime of the age was plotted after a couple of beers in the pub and involved nothing more technical than the ability to open a couple of doors and squeeze into a confined space. Sorry to disappoint, but that was the extent of it.

So how did my musing in the pub result in the appearance of three menacing hoodlums in my kitchen a few weeks later? I can only assume that word got around. East End pubs have ears, people listen in and speak to other people. I was known in the neighbourhood. I came from a well-known area. It wouldn't have been beyond the realms of possibility for my conversation to have been carried off through the underworld grapevine. There were several known crews whose associates drank in the boozer and those crews were always looking to recruit new blood and get involved in new projects. My theory, in all its simplicity, was too good to pass up. Plenty of people knew me. I was easy to find. And that's how I ended up with Mr Chatty, Scarface and Ratty helping themselves to the digestives in my biscuit tin and explaining what they were after.

'The thing is, Eddie, we know what you do and where you work. And we know that you are a smart bloke. We'd like to work with you on a little job. It'll make all of us a lot of money if we do it properly,' Mr Chatty explained. 'We know you know how to do it and we can make sure it goes off nice and easy. No one has to get hurt.'

And then he said something that chilled my blood.

'Debbie's a lovely lady, isn't she? You're a lucky man, aren't you? And little Lee. What a cutie. It would be awful if something ever happened to them.' He didn't have to explain what he meant.

'Are you threatening me?' I tried to sound aggressive but my voice quivered. All three of the men laughed.

Ratty piped up. 'You see, Eddie, the thing is we represent a group of very driven individuals,' he said, referring to his gangland bosses. 'They have a special interest in you because they know what you do and they know you know how to relieve your bosses of some of their cargo. They want to help you have a better life. If you do this little thing for them, you, Debbie and Lee can start again somewhere new. New life, new identity, plenty of money, no more shitty jobs, no more shitty debts. You'll be looked after. You really will be a mug if you don't do as you're told. You owe it to Debbie and the kid. Like we said, it would be a shame if anything happened to them.

Work with us, Eddie and they are all protected, but if you are not with us you are against us and we can't guarantee what will happen to any of you.'

That was how it was couched – it would be beneficial to me. They said they knew I drove the truck which delivered to the banks on the coast. They knew the drops and to this day I wonder whether they had another man on the inside who I didn't know about because they seemed to know the timings and routing.

'One day soon, next week maybe, we are going to ask you to do something for us,' Mr Chatty continued. 'After you do, we'll get you safely out of the country and you will have enough money to live comfortably. You're not stupid, Eddie. You breathe a word of this to anyone, including Debbie and we will fuck you up. Do you understand?' I nodded. The atmosphere was getting even more tense.

'You work with us and you'll be fine,' continued Ratty. 'God forbid, if you get caught, you'll be looked after and so will your family. If you go to prison, people in there will try and lean on you to find out where the money is. We'll make sure that doesn't happen, keep you comfortable and look after you when you get out.'

I got the impression they were pretty confident I would get caught and were setting me up as a patsy. I don't think they accounted for the fact that I can be very incognito if I want to be. Mr Chatty clapped his hands together. I jumped.

'So what do you say, Eddie? Are we business partners?'

I had no choice. I nodded reluctantly. 'OK,' I muttered.

'I knew you'd do the right thing,' Mr Chatty cracked a smile. 'We'll be in touch.'

The three of them walked out, leaving me standing alone in the kitchen with my heart racing, trying to get my head around what I'd just done. I had made a pact with the devil and sold my soul. I did it, guilty as charged. I am guilty. The theft was my idea, the method was my idea and I was the one who drove the van away eventually.

I sat down on the kitchen stool and tried to rationalise things. Why did I say yes? To protect my family. What if I said no? Bye-bye, Debbie, bye-bye, Lee. Why not go to the police? Because if these people were the sort of people I believed they were, the police were not going to protect me or my family. Then I weighed up the pros and cons. What could go wrong? I could get caught, I could go to jail. Debbie and Lee could disappear. What were the chances of getting caught? Pretty high. How long would I do jail? Maximum sentence for theft: five years. If it worked, what would I gain? Money, new life. What would I lose? Shit job, low prospects, growing debts.

When Debbie came home later that day I didn't say a word and tried to act normally. I was already trying to justify my decision in my head. It was a chance to start again and have a better life. I started thinking about where we could go. Spain was the obvious choice but I didn't speak Spanish and the prospect of living out my days in hiding on the Costa del Crime didn't appeal. The USA, on the other hand, seemed a real possibility. It was big enough to get lost in and we had both loved it when we went.

Over the following days I continued to work things out in my head. I got another visit two days after the first. Again Debbie was out. This time it was just Mr Chatty and Ratty. 'Scarface having his beauty sleep?' I said dryly as they pushed past me and went into the lounge to sit down. There was no pretence that it was anything other than a threatening, coercive, one-sided arrangement. They were not in the mood for jokes.

'Shut up and listen, Eddie,' said Mr Chatty. 'This is what will happen. In a few days from now you will get a call. The next day you will go into work and leave your car at home. You won't be going home after that. You will start your run as usual and we will be watching and following. At a certain point you will get the nod and you will follow us. That's how it will happen. It's simple. Do not fuck it up.'

'What happens then?' I asked.

'We get the money out of the van, what do you think happens?' he scoffed.

'To me. What happens to me?'

'You will be looked after. Leave that to us. We'll get you somewhere safe with your family.'

'I want to go to America. I'll only do it if you get me to America,' I blurted. It was a brazen move to call the shots but it was a gamble I had to take. Over the previous days I had started to realise that, although they were in command, I had a small degree of bargaining power. They needed me and it was in their best interests to keep me on-side. It was also in their best interests to get me as far away as possible, to a country where I'd be happy and less likely to get caught or start to make trouble for them in the future. The longer I was on the run, the better for them. I had already decided that I was going to get Debbie and Lee out of the country myself, before anything happened, and I needed to know that I'd be able to get to where I was sending them.

Mr Chatty looked shocked for a moment, then he laughed. 'Shouldn't be a problem,' he said, before the two of them got up and left.

Over the following days I started to scrabble together enough money for two tickets to the USA and I had to borrow some from my family. I had worked out a plan. Initially, I needed to go somewhere to lay low, away from places where there would be lots of Brits, so the east and west coasts and Florida were out of the question. For some reason I hit on Dallas. I looked on a map and Dallas jumped out. It was in the south, which was warmer and it was almost in the centre of the country. The only problem was that I only had enough for fares to Boston one-way. I needed to do some persuading but I bought the tickets anyway from a travel agent and worked out a story to tell Debbie, who was totally oblivious to what was going on.

Once I'd purchased the tickets I waited for the right opportunity and started to weave my web of deceit. In the course of life, I have learned that if you want to pass off a dodgy bit of news, you can deliver it in what people sometimes refer to as a shit sandwich. You sandwich the shitty filling in between two slices of good news.

Top slice.

'I've got a surprise, darling,' I said, over dinner. 'I got a bonus at work. We're going on holiday!'

'Really?' Debbie was suspicious. She knew we'd been struggling.

'Yeah, it's an employee profit-share thing. I've sorted a few bills out and there is enough left for us to get away.'

'Wow, that's brilliant news,' she said.

Shitty filling.

'The only problem is that I could only get tickets on stand-by, which means we go very soon. And I can't get time off straight away.'

'What are you trying to say?' Debbie frowned.

'That you'll have to go with Lee a few days earlier and I'll come out when I get time off.'

'No way!'

Bottom slice.

'It's the only way I could afford to get us to…' – I did a drum roll on the table – '…AMERICA!'

'Oh, my God! No way!' Debbie ate the shit sandwich.

'I always said we'd go back. It's the only way I could afford it and pay off a few bills,' I said. I felt terrible. I hated lying. The masterstroke was the mention of the USA. If I had tickets to Benidorm it would have been a harder sell.

As I went into the details Debbie wasn't too impressed. I explained that she could fly to Boston first because we had been there first and she liked it. She could spend some time there and then get on a train and head south where I'd meet her in Dallas a couple of weeks later. I'd looked at flight times and picked a flight I was going to tell the crooks I needed to be on. The two weeks would give me enough time to do whatever they wanted me to do and to get to the States. If I got there earlier I could lie low until Debbie arrived.

'The train is supposed to be the best way to see the country,' I explained.

I'm still not sure she was totally convinced but, when I need to be, I can be convincing and a few days later – to my huge relief – I waved her and Lee off at the airport. The first part of the plan had fallen into place. I was committed and there was no turning back. I tried not to think too hard about what I was doing because when I did I started to get palpitations and anxiety. I shoved it to the back of my mind. At best I gave myself a 50/50 chance of getting away with it in the short term but was convinced, like the people who were forcing me into it, that I'd get caught at some point. With Debbie out of the country I had one less thing to worry about.

After just a day on my own, fighting waves of paranoia, looking over my shoulder and trying to stay sane, I finally got the nod. I got a call in the evening.

'I see you've sent Debbie and Lee away,' the voice said. It was another underhand threat to let me know that they were keeping tabs on me and my family. I couldn't work out which, if any, of the men it was. 'Smart move. If all goes according to plan and if you behave yourself, you'll see them soon.'

'I've told them to meet me in Dallas in two weeks,' I explained. I gave them the day and the time of the flight I'd told Debbie to meet me from.

'You just worry about what you need to do to keep them safe,' said the man. 'It's happening this Friday.'

The phone went dead. I stayed there for a few seconds with the receiver held to my ear. I could hear the blood pumping in my ears over the buzz of the disconnection tone.

CHAPTER 7

HEIST

Friday 22 January 1993. The alarm went off at about 5am but I was already awake. I'd hardly slept a wink. The adrenaline and anxiety combined to ensure that I spent most of the night tossing around in bed, wide-eyed, mind racing. I was glad when the alarm sounded because I wanted the day to get going and to get it over and done with.

Normally, the 5am starts were a bind, but that day the earlier I could get out the better. I had ordered a cab the previous evening because I'd been told to leave my car at home. I wasn't hungry so I didn't eat breakfast. I made a coffee instead and put on the dark blue uniform. It had epaulettes on the shoulders that suggested the wearer had some form of military link. This made me laugh because a lot of the people who worked in cash in transit and other sectors of the private security business were retired military or frustrated military wannabes who were too unfit, old or medically unable to be real soldiers.

I knew that it was the last time I would be in the South Woodham Ferrers house. But it was a rental and had never felt like home. We had not put down proper roots since the pub and even that had never really felt like a home. Most of our stuff had to be replaced after the fire so we didn't have lots of gear with sentimental associations lying around. I took a last look in Lee's bedroom. His bed was neatly made. There was a shelf full of books Debbie read to him and a few toys scattered around the floor. He'd taken his favourites on 'holiday' and I told myself he'd have plenty more after I joined them in the US. I had to convince myself the plan would work, otherwise I wouldn't be able to go through with it.

In the lounge I removed a couple of family photos from their frames, folded them up and put them in my pocket. I was deep in thought when the sound of a car horn made me jump. I pulled back the curtains and looked outside. The taxi had arrived and without feeling any nostalgia I left the last UK house I'd live in for over 20 years.

The ride to work in Chelmsford was quiet, which suited me and the cab driver, who had either been working all night or had just started. He looked knackered and was clearly unimpressed at having to take a fare at such an ungodly hour.

It was cold and damp when I arrived at the depot just before 6am. There were several other guards already there, getting the last cup of tea or coffee in before loading the vans. I met my partner for the day, a bloke called Peter Bunn. He was around the same age as me and, like me, he'd also been in the military. He had been working for Securicor for many years and before that had served as a submariner, so long hours spent confined in the metal interior of an armoured vehicle was probably a home from home for him. That morning we met, we exchanged pleasantries and we went to get the van for the day.

No one chatted too much first thing and a lot of the old timers didn't bother to get to know the newer recruits too well because there was such a high turnover of staff. They didn't see the point in spending time getting to know someone who was unlikely to stick around for more than a few months.

In his subsequent statement Peter said that I didn't appear nervous in any way. I must have been a great actor because I was crapping myself. And although I made a point of trying to be as congenial as possible, I couldn't say too much because my mouth was completely dry. I was so nervous my tongue was stuck to the roof of my mouth and several times I tried to say things to keep an easy flow of conversation but only mumbles came out in place of words.

The vans were parked in a bay in the depot and the first one we were assigned didn't start. We got keys for another and that seemed to be working. It was a dark blue, armoured two-tonne Ford Transit. It was three years old and the same as most of the other vans: diesel, heavy and a bit of a pig to drive. It was fitted with a two-way radio system which allowed the driver and the delivery guard – or bag man – to keep in contact. It also had a state-of-the-art tracking system, one of the first ones ever developed. In theory, Datatrak allowed the control centre back at base to keep tabs on where the van was at all times. In reality, both the radio and the tracking systems had lots of glitches and were patchy at best.

Because Peter was the most senior, he was the bag man. It was the more responsible and technical of the jobs and so it made sense for the more experienced member of the crew to do it. I realised how convenient it was that I was the driver that day and wondered if my puppet-masters knew it too.

We climbed in the van and Peter put his flask, packed lunch, pipe and tobacco in the cab. 'Not got any sandwiches today, Eddie?' he asked.

'No, I'll get something after the round,' I said, as casually as I could. I wasn't expecting to be around for long.

We went to the vault where the delivery had already been counted out and was waiting for us, wrapped in opaque cellophane and packed into kit bags. It was a big delivery of around 50 bags, each of which contained around £25,000. The cargo consisted of payday money and money for the weekend so was bigger than normal. Again I wondered at how much inside knowledge the people controlling me had. If you were going to hit a specific route on a specific day, the route we were on that day would certainly yield a decent result. We loaded the cash into the van, signed for it and drove out of the vault and out at the depot just as I had done many times over the past five months. The whole process took over an hour and we headed for Suffolk and the drab seafront port of Felixstowe. The journey would take over an hour through rush hour.

There wasn't a great deal of conversation on the way. There never was. I'd worked with Peter the previous week but even though we'd been cooped up in the van together for hours, we didn't know much about each other. He seemed perfectly nice but we didn't have much in common and weren't destined to be lifelong friends. He said later that I wasn't chatty. I was shaking like a leaf and paranoid that I'd put a foot wrong so I wasn't in the mood for deep discussions. I can't recall exactly what we said – I probably talked about the football. I was so nervous and anxious that day that some of the events have been lost in my memory. I was on autopilot and all I could think about was Debbie and Lee and going through with what I had to do to keep them safe.

We had one stop to make first at a post office on the route to Felixstowe. As we got nearer to the destination my heart beat faster and faster. I could feel my face getting hot and started to worry that Peter would notice something was wrong. I was convinced whatever was going to happen would happen early. But the post office stop, when we delivered money and collected some, went without a hitch.

Just before 9.30am I pulled up outside that Lloyd's Bank in Hamilton Road, Felixstowe, on time for the drop. The doors were shut and the bank was closed. Protocol stated that we couldn't wait outside a closed bank with a case full of money so we had to sit and wait until the doors opened. We exchanged a few words and I started to think about things. All the way I had been looking in my rear-view mirror to see if I was being followed. If I was I could not tell. I had no idea when I would be given the signal or what the signal would be. What if it had already been given and I didn't recognise it? I started to panic. There was an old man hanging around by the side of the van; what if he was the signal? Did I need to speak to him? I looked in the wing mirrors. Was he one of the gangsters in disguise? Was there some kind of code I needed to know? I started to sweat. Peter's voice snapped me out of my paranoid train of thought.

'I think it's open,' he said. 'Someone's just gone in, I'll go and check.'

I let him out and watched as he walked to the front door to check. He turned around and gave the thumbs-up so I went into the back of the van and loaded the delivery into the case. There were two bags earmarked for the bank but rules meant that he could only take one at a time. I placed the case into the chute and, at 9.30am, Peter Bunn took the container out of the other side and turned his back on Securicor Ford Transit van, registration number H485 OAX. I got back in the driver's cab and watched him walk a few yards across the pavement and through the arch that led to the doors of the bank. He went in and I waited no more than 30 seconds before my own beat – up Opel Ascona pulled alongside me. Ratty was at the wheel. Mr Chatty was in the passenger seat. He looked at me and pointed straight ahead in a gesture that plainly meant 'Follow us'.

'Here we go,' I breathed to myself and gunned the engine.

The getaway was, most likely, the most mundane, uneventful getaway in the history of bank jobs. I eased very carefully out into the traffic behind the Opel, which was being driven equally carefully. The van, as I mentioned, was a pig to drive.

It had a notional top speed of 70 mph that would only have been achievable after an hour driving down a steep slope. The gangster duo were smart enough to realise that armoured trucks don't go fast and they didn't want to lose me so we tootled through Felixstowe like pensioners. My hand was shaking on the wheel. I knew we had limited time. The Datatrak was supposed to connect each van to a control room and alert them when the van deviated from its route. This was the early stages of that kind of technology and I wasn't sure how it worked and whether it gave the person monitoring it a real-time record of where the van was. But Securicor was very proud of its revolutionary system and used it as a selling point. Had I known how hit-and-miss it was and that the van wouldn't be located for another 45 minutes I would have relaxed a little more. There was also an alarm inside the van, but I was disinclined to activate it.

We drove down a main road to the seafront and turned left onto the main seafront road. It was surreal. We passed amusement arcades, the council offices and the pier. I wondered if they knew where they were going and then started to wonder if there was a boat waiting somewhere for us. After half a mile the road became less built up. On one side there was a row of brightly coloured beach huts. It was quiet everywhere. The amusement arcades were all shut and it was the wrong time of year for visitors.

I was concentrating hard on sticking to the speed limit and driving normally. The radio made me jump. Peter's voice crackled out of the speakers.

'Eddie?' he said. 'Eddie… where are you?'

I ignored it.

A minute later he came over the radio again, this time fainter. 'Er, Eddie? Have you been moved on by traffic wardens? Eddie?'

Poor Peter had a long day after that. He was dragged in for questioning and wasn't released until late at night. After he realised I was gone he went back into the bank where he called the control room in Chelmsford and told them the van had gone. There was general confusion until, at 9.38am, someone dialled 999. Peter couldn't even have a smoke. His pipe, tobacco, sarnies and flask were in the van with me. He got a letter from the police 20 years later when I was finally jailed that thanked him for his help. All he did was get out of the van, walk into the bank and then come out and be left standing on the pavement. Well done, Peter Bunn!

Anyway, after what seemed like ages but was only a few minutes, I followed the Ascona past Mannings Amusement Park – a run-down, depressing collection of rides, crazy golf and themed attractions – then turned right into Micklegate Road, a quiet, residential street. There was an empty car park on one side and the equally empty amusement park on the other. A few yards up, my gangster partners parked adjacent to the side of a 'Crazy House' attraction and a row of trees. I pulled up behind them. Chatty jumped out of the Ascona and ran to the side of the van, which he knocked on. From my position in the driving seat I let him in using the buzzer. He knew his way around the system. He used the key Peter had left in the door to open the inner door which led to the back of the van and the money. He told me to get in the back with him.

'Start loading,' he ordered. I did. At that point I was as complicit in the whole caper as they were. I'd driven away, I was as guilty as them so I did as they said because it was in my best interests to make the scheme work.

We loaded the bags into the airlock as quickly as we could. There was no time to stack neatly; we tossed every bag into it, stacking them in a mess against the far side. There were bags of money all over the place.

'Leave the coins,' Mr Chatty ordered. I tossed them aside and several bags split.

It took less than two minutes to load what the police and Securicor said was £1.2 million into the airlock. I never counted it so I can't be sure what the exact figure was. Once it was all in Mr Chatty, who was breathing heavily, puffed: 'Get in,' and gestured to the airlock. I understood what was happening. We were both getting in with the money. I squeezed in as close to the far side as I could, crushed against bags of loot. He pushed in too, his back crushing against my front. He took the key from the interior door, closed it and locked it. Then he shuffled around so we were face to face, pressed against each other, and reached around me to unlock the outer door. It popped open and we both fell out.

Ratty was waiting outside and immediately started unloading the money into my car, stuffing bags in the boot and the footwells at the back. No one walked past or drove past. At the end of the road cars continued to pass, oblivious of what was happening a few yards away. It took around 30 seconds to transfer the money into the Opel – the world's crappiest getaway vehicle. In hindsight, however, their choice was inspired. It was such a nondescript heap of rubbish that it melted into the traffic. They got in the front, I took my jumper, tie and name badge off and got in the back as they started the engine and drove off, leaving the van empty, except for a load of coins scattered all over the place.

We drove back down to the seafront and along to a car park. We pulled in and I saw Scarface standing by the side of a weird-looking people carrier, the type favoured by pensioners, mums and people with dogs. He was trying to look incognito but failing miserably, mainly because he was such an ugly lump.

'Grab the bags and put them in the Previa,' Ratty ordered.

'The what?' I said.

'The fucking Previa,' he hissed – it was a Toyota Previa and I still remember it.

I didn't argue. I was shaking with adrenaline and my mouth was dry again. I did notice that there were a few people wandering past but no one seemed to think there was anything unusual about three blokes transferring several bulky kit bags from one vehicle to another.

Once the money was loaded, Scarface told me to get in the passenger side. He got in the driver's seat and we drove off, leaving the other two to dispose of the Ascona. I discovered later that it was found a few miles away, burned out. Shame, I have sentimental memories of that motor.

Scarface let out a sigh of relief. 'Nice job,' he said. 'You'd better get in the footwell, they'll be looking for you.' I wasn't in the mood to chat. I think I went into shock. I slunk down and tried to think nice thoughts. I thought of Debbie and Lee and the life we were going to have.

CHAPTER 8

GETAWAY

In the initial confusion following the robbery, the police had been concerned that I'd been kidnapped, even though they knew it was unlikely someone could get in the van without being let in by the driver. Why they thought I'd let kidnappers in I'll never know, but any foolishness on their behalf gave me more of a chance to escape so I'm glad they followed that line of investigation.

Crouched in the footwell of the car, I had no idea that there were several things working in my favour. Firstly, it took the police around 45 minutes to finally locate the van – it having turned out that Datatrak was Datacrap. The all-singing, all-dancing system that Securicor boasted about was as useful as a chocolate teapot. When police eventually found the van they couldn't get in it because the outer door of the airlock was locked. They had to get someone from Securicor to open it up for them. They were expecting to see me tied up in the back of it, beaten up and gagged. Instead, there was no one.

I sometimes like to imagine the look on the faces of the first cops who got in. They would have been confronted by a space empty except for several hundred coins scattered all over the place. My mum would have been really angry with me because there were a lot of 50 pence pieces on that run and she used to religiously collect 50 pences for the gas meter. We all had to save our 50 p's to keep the boiler going. She could have had free gas for life with all the coins we left behind. I can hear her now: 'What a flipping waste.'

Meanwhile, from my hiding place in a Japanese space wagon with the secret love-child of Jaws from the James Bond movies and Jason Statham by my side, I started to contemplate what I'd just done. I knew we'd taken a lot of money; the back of the car was full of it. I didn't realise just how much or that, at the time, it was one of the biggest heists in criminal history, but I knew I was in trouble and I knew there was no turning back. In for a penny, in for a million pounds, as they say! I was fighting hard to keep the panic in check. I was a passenger in more ways than one. I was totally at the mercy of the men who had forced me into the job and I was reliant on them to keep me hidden and get me out. I knew it was in their best interests to make sure I didn't caught because it meant there was less chance of them getting arrested. While it was in my DNA never to grass, they didn't know that. We were in it together and they needed to keep me sweet. I couldn't turn back what I had done, I was committed. There hadn't been a lot of honour on their behalf as they'd threatened my family, but we were business partners in an enterprise that we all stood a lot to gain or lose from. We were mutually reliant.

I had no idea where we were going because I dared not sit up. We seemed to be driving for ages when the car came to a halt and the engine stopped. My back was screaming out in pain and my legs had gone dead. 'You can get out now,' Scarface said. 'Follow me, keep your head down and don't speak to anyone. We're going into a block of flats. They are just next to the car. I'll tell you when the coast is clear.'

He took a quick look around, opened his door and said: 'Right, come on, quickly.' I struggled to get out of my position. My back creaked and one foot was completely numb and so I struggled to climb out, before limping after Scarface like Quasimodo. I learned later that I needn't have made such an effort to hide. The police, in their infinite wisdom, didn't tell the media about the theft until later in the afternoon and they only released details then because a member of the public had tipped off a local paper that something big had happened in Felixstowe.

Scarface walked around to the back of the car, opened the boot, pulled out a bag, locked the door and beckoned for me to follow him into the foyer of the flats we'd pulled up alongside. For some reason I knew we were in London – maybe it was the smell – and I suspected we were in the east, but I wasn't too sure where.

'I hope the lock's OK on that car,' I said as we walked to a staircase at the far end of a concrete corridor lined by identical blue doors. It occurred to me that any opportunist car thief who fancied a quick smash and grab would have the result of their life. We were in a low-rise council block. It was the type I'd attended hundreds of times when I was a fireman. It smelled damp and it was cold. 'Where are we?' I asked.

'Wapping. There's a flat here for you to lie low in,' he explained, 'and don't worry about the car. It's being watched.'

We climbed up two floors and along a corridor to a door which he opened with a key. At the time Wapping was a mixed area of residential and industrial properties to the east of the City of London. Half of it was renovated warehouse apartments full of yuppies, half of it was council flats. It had the benefit of being quiet. Most of the residents worked in London so during the days it was empty, despite its proximity to the centre of the capital. The main industry was News International's printing works, which had been the scene of a long-running, often violent industrial dispute in the 1980s between Rupert Murdoch's media empire, backed by Margaret Thatcher and striking printers, backed by the unions. But the striking printers had long gone and the plant remained. It was home to a huge printing hall and also to the offices of the *Sun*, the *News of the World*, *The Times* and the *Sunday Times*. I wonder now how all those journalists would feel if they knew the biggest story in the country was hiding out under their noses.

Once inside the flat, Scarface revealed more of the plan. 'You need to stay here until we can get you out. We're working on getting you to your family. People will be looking for you so you need to be quiet and not draw attention to yourself. Only go out if you absolutely have to and, if you do go out, go in the day, keep your head down, wear a cap and stay away from people because if you get caught you are on your own and you know what will happen to your family if you ever talk. The best thing you can do is stay here and keep your mouth shut. There's stuff for you in here and food in the kitchen. We'll be watching and we'll be back.' He dumped the bag he was carrying on the floor.

'See you later then,' I said sarcastically. He turned and left, shutting the door gently behind him, so as not to make too much noise.

The thing I remember was the silence. For a block of flats in a city, it was remarkably quiet. Every now and then you could hear a door shutting somewhere, or the low murmur of a television, but apart from that there were hardly any cars passing and hardly any people on the street outside.

I looked around the flat. The front door opened to a small corridor, there was a toilet to one side, a cupboard on the other and a door to the lounge directly in front. The lounge was sparsely furnished with a cloth sofa and armchair, a sideboard, a table and chairs and a TV. On one side there was a kitchen with Formica units, an old standalone oven with electric hob and a fridge. I looked in the cupboards. There were loads of tins. Beans, pies, corned beef, tinned spaghetti, tinned tomatoes. It was like someone had stocked up for a war. In the fridge there were the basics: milk, butter, a few carrots, potatoes. There was bread in a bread tin and another two loaves and some oven chips and frozen pizza in the small freezer above the fridge. The bedroom had one bed in it, a chair, a cheap chest of drawers and an empty, new suitcase. There was soap, shampoo, a new toothbrush and toothpaste in the bathroom along with some disposable razors. The whole place was depressing.

I walked back into the living room and picked up the bag Scarface had left for me. I put it on the table and opened it. There were several changes of clothes in it, all in my size. There was also a suit and, bizarrely, a huge pair of thick glasses. I looked at them and frowned. They looked like something you'd buy in a joke shop. There were also two bundles of money which I counted. There was £5,000 – emergency funds to keep me sweet, I assumed. They didn't give me my cut because they needed to keep me under control and withholding the money was a way of making sure I didn't wander off.

I slept in that flat for over a week and it was like purgatory, cooking beans on toast and watching the news. The days drifted into each other. I broke the monotony by doing exercises, lying on the floor and doing sit-ups and push-ups. I set myself targets, 100 one day, 150 the next and so on. In the end I was doing 600 sit-ups a day and 600 push-ups. I kept the money close by all the time. When I went to bed I kept it under the pillow in case the cops came in and I needed to leg it. I hardly slept. I felt like I was sealed inside a coffin at times. The last thing I needed was time to think about what had happened but that was all I had and every scenario went through my mind. What if Debbie had heard the news and decided to leave me? What if she'd come back to the UK and had been arrested? I didn't even know where she and Lee were. I went a bit delirious at times. Every time I heard footsteps outside I stuffed the money in my pocket and got ready to fight my way out of the flat. I was on edge constantly and it was exhausting.

Meanwhile, outside, I was becoming the biggest story in the country. I got to watch it all unfold on the TV in the lounge. Despite the police's initial reluctance to admit what had happened, one of the evening papers in East Anglia managed to get a special edition out on the day about the '£1 million bank raid'. Police said they were withholding details because they were still concerned that I had been kidnapped. But they issued a press statement giving the bare bones of the story in which they got the name of the road where the van was dumped wrong, diverting attention away from an area where there could have been witnesses and giving me another advantage.

On Saturday the story hit the TV news and the national press. A figure of £700,000 was quoted, which was news to me. The newspapers were full of speculation. The *Sun* screamed 'Guard does a runner with £1 million, The *Daily Mail* told readers I was 'Missing with a million pounds'. There was speculation that I'd fled the country because there were several ferry services from Felixstowe to the continent and there was also speculation that Debbie and Lee were being held hostage somewhere. I was painted as the criminal mastermind behind a meticulously plotted, audacious crime.

By Sunday my photo was all over the news. It was on every news report on every channel. The good old *News of the World* ran a false story claiming that I'd been involved in a raid before. Unknown to me, reporters started to hound my family, who for the most part kept quiet but did do their best to try and counter the false image that was being built up of me. Instead, they told reporters I was a decent bloke and I wasn't grumpy! Apart from a few comments refuting the crap that was being generated my family did what people from our neck of the woods always did – they looked after their own and kept schtum.

In some ways it would have been funny, if I hadn't been the main character in the story that was being constructed – all the details were coming out wrong and were being embellished. Apparently, I had discussed moving to the USA and opening a flying school; I was a trained locksmith; I had gambling debts. It was all sensationalised and skewed. After several days there was speculation that police had already gone to the US.

Then someone coined the name 'Fast Eddie', along with the spelling mistake and it stuck. It all became very surreal. It was like watching a film where I was a character, but I didn't recognise myself. At one point someone even managed to get the train robber Ronnie Biggs to comment. He was still on the lam in Brazil. He said, 'I hope he gets away with it and I'm sure most of the British people would be behind him.' And that was the strange thing that I started to become aware of as I watched the story gain momentum from my hideout. It became progressively apparent that the public were rooting for me. No one had been hurt and the only victims were the banks and a huge security company and, ultimately, the insurance company that would have to pay out. For many people it was a victimless crime and they enjoyed the idea that I'd stuck two fingers up at the corporations and was winning. I was like Robin Hood, except I wasn't robbing from the rich to give to the poor. I stole from the rich and gave it to the crooks who made me do it. But you can't let the details get in the way of a good story, can you?

The police investigation was given the name of Operation Ramble, which was apt because it did appear to lack any real focus. There were 30 officers assigned to catch me. All forces in the UK were alerted and ports and airports were told to keep an eye out in case I attempted to slip out of the country. Interpol was supplied with the details of me and Debbie. Within days there was a £50,000 reward offered – slightly less than the £700,000 first mentioned in the press – and then, a week later, some bright spark realised that, given the amount of money that had gone missing, the people behind the heist could easily pay off anyone tempted to claim £50,000 so the reward was doubled. Police started working on the assumption that there may have been more than one person involved, which strangely made me feel a bit better. At least they recognised I wasn't the only one. The media still focused on Fast Eddie though.

On Monday, Operation Ramble released Debbie's details and mentioned that once she had worked in Essex police control room as a 999 operator. They also gave details of the Previa which, bizarrely, had been found back in Felixstowe and also of my Ascona, which was found burned out in Essex six days after the theft. On 3 February Suffolk police issued a statement that sounded suspiciously like a cover-up for their lack of progress, leads or information. It said they had pursued more than 500 lines of inquiry and interviewed more than 450 people in 15 countries. Despite that they had squat and they were getting increasingly frustrated.

Somewhere in the middle of my period of enforced absence I was taken on a trip. Mr Chatty arrived. He let himself in with a key. As soon as I heard someone at the door I panicked, grabbed the money and ran to hide in the cupboard in the front hall. I had worked out an escape plan – I was going to wait until any intruder was in the lounge and then make a dash for it. My plan fell at the first hurdle however because Mr Chatty was through the door before I could get to the cupboard. I met him face to face in the hall. To be honest, I hadn't been paying much attention to personal hygiene and I hadn't shaved for days. I looked like a wild animal, half-crouching, wide-eyed with fear, clutching a bundle of notes.

Mr Chatty looked at me and laughed genuinely for the first time since we met. I was so relieved that it was him I started laughing too. 'Jesus, mate, you look like shit,' he laughed.

'I think I've had a coronary,' I answered.

'We've got something to do. You'll be pleased to know that we're going on a little trip. Go and clean yourself up, put something smart on and bring the glasses,' he said.

I did as he said and nervously left the flat for the first time in over a week. He had a car parked outside. 'We need to get some passport photos done,' he explained. 'We're working on getting you out of the country like we said. I take it you've seen you're all over the news?'

'Yeah, I saw a couple of snippets,' I said wryly.

'Fast Eddie!' he said, shaking his head. We both laughed again and he told me to keep my head down.

He took me to a nearby station which was quiet and which had a photo booth just inside the entrance. With the glasses on and several day's stubble on my face I felt quite confident that I wouldn't get recognised. Cities are perfect places in which to disappear and no one took any notice. It took a couple of minutes and I waited in the booth until the strip was developed while Mr Chatty waited outside. Once the machine had spat them out, he took them and we walked back to the car.

'Back to the hotel,' he said.

'Great,' I sighed.

'It won't be long now. If all goes well, the next time we meet you'll be on your way,' he reassured.

Back in Wapping the days dragged by. It was another week before Mr Chatty came by again and I was getting increasingly anxious because the date of the flight I'd given Debbie was almost upon me. It was an evening and he was in a good mood. He had a bag in his hand.

'I've got a present for you, Eddie,' he said, 'or should that be Stephen? Meet the new you.' He pulled out a passport and threw it on the table. I picked it up and opened it. Inside there was one of the photographs from our trip to the booth. The name on the passport was 'Stephen King'.

'Are you kidding me?' I said. 'Stephen King, like the American author that everyone knows. I thought I was supposed to be incognito. Couldn't you have picked something less well known?'

'Sorry, mate,' he shrugged, 'you can't really pick and choose identities. It doesn't work like that.' Then I saw the issue date – it started in a month's time. 'Don't worry about that,' he said. 'They only ever look at the expiry date. If they ask, tell them you applied for a renewal in advance before your old one expired and it came through with that date in it. Happens all the time.' He pulled a plane ticket from the bag. 'Tomorrow, Dallas,' he said. 'It's the flight you wanted. There'll be a car to pick you up and take you to Heathrow.'

I allowed myself the luxury of a smile and some optimism. The crazy plan was going to work. I was going to see my family. I glanced at the ticket. It was for a United Airlines flight to Dallas from Heathrow the following evening. It was business class.

'You'll need to wear the suit,' Mr Chatty said. 'Business is better, they tend to ask less questions, there are fewer people, smaller queues. Don't worry about the extra expense, we took it from your cut.'

He slid the bag across the table to me. I looked inside. There were five fat wads of money inside. They looked like the £25,000 bundles from the Securicor delivery. Which meant £125,000. All the way through I hadn't known what cut I was getting. It was left to their generosity. They had to give me enough to make it easy for me to disappear. I did some quick mental arithmetic. The money would certainly allow me to go underground for a while when you took into account the exchange rate, but I knew and he knew that it wouldn't last forever.

He read my thoughts and shrugged. 'There were a few stakeholders who needed to get paid,' he said. It was obvious there was no negotiation. I can't be sure, but it almost seemed as though he felt bad about what was a stitch-up. I'd been given just enough to keep me quiet and to give me a shot at a clean getaway. They probably assumed I'd disappear for a couple of years until it run out or I got caught, during which time they'd dissolve back into the underworld they emerged from.

Mr Chatty held out his hand. 'This is us done then Eddie, nice doing business with you,' he said.

I shook it. 'I hope we don't meet again,' I said.

He smiled, turned around and walked away. 'Don't worry about tidying the place up. We'll get housekeeping round when you've gone,' he called out as he left.

The following day I packed the clothes into the suitcase and wrapped the bundles of cash carefully in some towels. The money would have to go into the hold. It was the luck of the draw whether it got checked but at that stage I had no choice and airport security in the early 1990s was much more basic. Customs were more concerned with people smuggling bottles of spirits and cartons of cigarettes.

In the late afternoon a minicab arrived. I watched it pull up through the net curtains. The driver came up and knocked on the door. I put on the ridiculous glasses. 'Mr King?' he said.

I nodded. Thankfully he didn't speak much English so the journey to Heathrow through heavy traffic was largely silent.

I checked in the suitcase without a problem. The business-class ticket was a masterstroke. There was no queue and staff were polite and focused on getting me through to the business lounge with the minimum of fuss. The most nerve-wracking part was walking through passport control. I handed the bloke my passport and tried my best not to look guilty. I was aware that every passport handler would have been shown my photo at some point over the previous weeks. He glanced at me and waved me through. I let out the breath I'd been holding. It was going to work. I was through.

I spent a nervous hour in the departure lounge and, as soon as the flight was called, I made my way to the gate. Stepping aboard the 747 to Dallas was like taking a step on the moon. I felt weightless. I settled into the reclining seat. For the first time since I'd been singled out to do the job I felt happy. When the plane accelerated along the runway and left the ground, I smiled. I was leaving my old life behind and had a chance to start a new one.

People think I went over to the US with £1.2 million. I had enough to give myself a start but no more. On the plane I started to try and work out how I was going to make it work when I got there and I had no idea. But like everything in life,

I had faith I'd find some way of making a go of things. For the time being I sat back and looked forward to being reunited with what I expected would be a very angry Debbie.

CHAPTER 9

DEBBIE IN THE USA

'Shush, please, Debbie, just try and keep your voice down. I'll explain everything.'

Debbie took the news as well as I would have expected. We were in the arrivals lounge of Dallas Fort Worth International airport and were in the midst of our tearful reunion. It was emotional for all the wrong reasons.

My first mistake was wearing the glasses. I thought I wouldn't be recognised while I was wearing them. It worked for Superman! I was so focused on getting through passport control and getting the suitcase that I forgot I was wearing them.

The airport was busy but the queue to the passport booths was mercifully short. I was one of only about ten people; business-class passengers get their own lane. The immigration bloke at the front of the queue was checking passports and asking random people questions. I shuffled forward and got nearer to the front. When it was my turn I stepped forward and handed him Stephen King's passport.

'What's the purpose of your visit, sir, business or pleasure?'

I'm wearing a suit and travelling business class – take a wild guess, I thought to myself. But sarcasm wouldn't work so I played along. 'A bit of both. I'm here to see if there is an opportunity to set up a business and invest.' It was half-true. There was a case, hopefully, waiting for me with five wads of money in it that I couldn't take back to the UK so it was destined for the US economy.

'What business are you in Mr King?' he said.

'Photocopier sales,' I said.

He nodded and handed me back the passport. 'Have a good trip,' he said.

I'd devised the photocopier sales story on the plane. I needed something boring, feasible and mundane that would ensure people wouldn't pry. If I made up something exciting or glamorous, they'd ask questions. Photocopiers were boring, no one was going to ask me to tell them all about my copier business. It had worked and I felt pleased with myself as I walked to baggage reclaim and my next small triumph. After a nervous, ten-minute wait, in which it seemed as though everyone else's bag came out first, I spotted my suitcase emerge from the bowels of the airport. There were no security stickers and it looked intact. I've never been so glad to see a bag come around on a carousel in my life. I grabbed it and walked through the 'Nothing to declare' channel.

I had arranged to meet Debbie in Dallas two weeks before and I still wasn't sure she'd be there. But I hadn't realised while I was in Wapping, watching the saturation of news stories about my crime, that the story actually had very little international appeal. It was a big story in the UK but elsewhere there were more important things happening and the US media had little interest in foreign news that didn't directly affect Americans. When Debbie saw me walk through the sliding doors in my silly specs she knew nothing about the job.

Her first words were along the lines of, 'Why are you wearing comedy glasses?'

'It's so good to see you,' I said, hastily pulling the glasses off and hugging her. Lee was asleep in a buggy. 'I need to tell you something.'

'Eddie, what's wrong?'

Women have a sixth sense that tells them when their men have done something wrong and Debbie's had gone into overdrive. There was a look of panic on her face. I'd had weeks to prepare for this moment and during the flight I repeatedly rehearsed the words I was going to use to bring her life crashing down. In that moment, I forgot them all. I felt burning shame and guilt for what I was about to put her and our son through. No number of shit sandwiches would make what I was about to tell her all right.

'You know we spoke about moving here and starting a new life?' She looked puzzled and nodded.

'Well, we can. The only problem is you can never speak to your family and I can never speak to mine again.'

The anger started bubbling under like lava in a volcano. 'What the hell have you done?' Her voice was rising.

That's when I asked her to keep her voice down. 'We need to go somewhere quiet. It's really important.'

We found a quiet corner away from the crowds and in a quiet voice, in case we were overheard, I explained to her that I had been forced to steal a security van filled with money, that she and Lee had been in danger and that I was a fugitive with a new identity and enough money to start anew. Even as I said it I realised how completely fantastical it sounded. It was like the storyline from a movie, but Debbie knew me better than anyone and she knew by the look on my face that I was telling the truth. She started to cry.

'We'll go to the police,' she said.

'No way! I did it. I'll go straight to jail.'

'But you were forced into it,' she argued.

'Do you think the courts and police will bother about that? We have a chance here, Debbie. We have money. The fact that you've not heard about it suggests that the police have no idea where I am. We'll lie low and enjoy life. We deserve it. How many people save all their lives and then die as soon as they retire? Loads. We can enjoy a retirement while we are still young enough. We can do all the things we always dreamed of and raise Lee somewhere where he'll have a better life.'

I'm a very fortunate bloke. Debbie loves me. Even before 1993, we'd been through a lot of crap together and came out the other side. We had always stuck together, through thick and thin and that glue held now. It didn't take too long for

Debbie to accept her new situation. The money helped a bit; we had a chance at a better lifestyle and were starting from scratch, as opposed to being under financial pressure. It was a clean break. We didn't have that much but we had enough to give ourselves a fresh start.

'Oh, Eddie, what are we going to do?' she said.

My normal response to any difficult challenge in life was always the same: it'll be OK, I'll sort it out. That's what I told her. 'Trust me, we'll be fine.' Understandably, she was worried about her family. She had sisters and although they weren't especially close, she was concerned about what they would be thinking watching the news in the UK.

I shook my head. 'You can't get in touch with them for quite some time. We can't speak to any of our family. It wouldn't be fair to drag them into this. It's my mess, Debbie, but all I care about is you and Lee and keeping you safe.'

To this day I feel guilty about putting Debbie through what I did and about distancing her from our family. I've felt guilty every day since and been trying to make it up to her for the last 20 years.

In the end we hugged and made a vow that we'd stick together, like we had always done. In the back of my mind I thought I'd be caught fairly quickly and I was constantly looking around me waiting for a tap on the shoulder or for someone to recognise me. That feeling lasted for several years. I had nothing planned for the long term. My immediate concern was to change some money up, which I did without problems at the airport and to get somewhere safe to stay. I didn't have a driver's licence so I couldn't rent a car, which was a problem. All I had was the passport. We took a taxi to a motel near the Six Flags Over Texas theme park and the next day we went there, like any other family on holiday. We were like a couple of grown-up kids and Debbie started to thaw. I was fairly confident that there wouldn't be many British people there. Dallas wasn't on the map as far as British tourists were concerned and it was February. Sure enough we didn't hear another British voice all the time we were there and enjoyed the rides and attractions without incident.

In the following days, I did some research. I called government departments and banks, I went to a library and looked up the rules and regulations around getting a driver's licence and other forms of ID. I read up on buying property and changing money. I used the same cover story that I used in the airport. I was Stephen King, a UK businessman who had sold a company in the UK and was on an extended stay in the US, enjoying the fruits of the sale and looking at other business possibilities. Everything else I decided to keep the same; the more lies I told, the more likely I was to get caught out. So when we were in a restaurant and the waitress asked what part of the UK we were from I told her Essex and east London. If people delved further I said I had been a fireman and had retired through injury. I gave people just enough information to satisfy them.

I made regular trips to different banks to change up as much as possible and started to build up a fund of dollars. I made sure I never went in the same bank twice and took every opportunity to change as much as I could. The passport held up to scrutiny. Within a week we had rented an apartment in a gated community in a suburb near Six Flags that had a concierge. We lay low and relaxed. I took every precaution I could think of. The weather was mild but I always wore sleeves to hide the tattoos that were a distinguishing feature and could help in identification. In fact, in every photograph over the following 20 years I was wearing long sleeves. I grew a moustache which I couldn't stand and tried a beard but that didn't last long. I dyed my hair too but it didn't take. I wore my glasses when I was out.

Dallas was a decent place, full of cattle ranchers, oil workers and farmers and I had every intention of staying for more than a few weeks. However, nature worked against us. With a growing fund of dollars and increased confidence I started to realise that we didn't have to lie low and hide, like fugitives. No one really seemed to be bothering us so as long as we were careful it made more sense to move around. I worried that if we stayed in one place for too long we'd increase the risk of getting caught. The more I learned about the US, the more I realised that it would be easy to travel. Domestic flights operated like buses at the time. You didn't need ID. As long as you had cash you could buy a car or a house. With a passport it was easy to get a driver's licence and with a licence you could get other forms of ID. They didn't ask too many questions. America was all about freedom; the whole system was set up against surveillance and the intrusion of government. It was the home of the free and the easiest place in the world to hide in plain sight.

One night I was sitting inside the apartment, watching TV when something landed on the back of my neck. I jumped off my seat and reached around my head to grab whatever it was. I pulled it off and looked closely. It was a huge, chocolate-coloured, beetle-like bug that flapped its wings as I held it between my thumb and forefinger.

'What the hell is this?' I said to Debbie, who was hiding behind a cushion. Then I realised. It was a cockroach. I've seen plenty of them in my life but that thing was bigger than my thumb. I threw it out the window in disgust and went downstairs to the concierge. I was appalled but there were other people with her and I didn't want to embarrass her so I quietly tried to whisper to her that there were 'roaches in the apartment and that we needed to get it fumigated straight away.

She laughed. 'You're in Texas now, honey, you better get used to them. They are everywhere. We can send in an exterminator tomorrow if you like but they will be back within a week.'

Up to that point I'd only been toying with the idea of moving on but that 'roach sealed the deal and made my mind up for me. I knew we weren't going to stay in Texas. It might have been no big deal to them but I came from England where 'roach infestations close down restaurants. Debbie agreed – she wasn't a fan of creepy-crawlies either. Over the following days we started to look for somewhere else to live.

In my research trips to the library I had been using the computers and had come across a program called Best Places that allowed me to set criteria and search for the best place to live in the US based on my requirements. It was a brilliant tool because it allowed us to get a good idea of a place without having to travel there. I started looking for places that would suit our lifestyle. Quiet, fairly remote, lots of leisure activity nearby, no British, no tourist industry, low crime rate, good schools.

One of the options that came up was Colorado. I liked the look of the state: it was rugged, it had good links but it wasn't on the tourist trail and it had the sort of community we could live in but who lived far enough away from each other so as not to be in each other's pockets. We had nothing to lose so we decided to give it a go. Our possessions fitted into two suitcases and we left our apartment and headed to Dallas airport, where we bought three one-way tickets and boarded our first internal flight to Colorado Springs. Once again we found a motel and started looking around for somewhere to rent. We found a short-term rental apartment and a few days later I bought my first car. Eventually, I also opened a bank account using the passport. Initially, I only put a few hundred dollars in it, just in case the ID alerted a security system somewhere. However, this was in the days before technology joined everything up. People still used cheques and cash and after a couple of weeks I realised that Stephen King was not going to set off any alarms in the banking system. Correspondence from the bank also acted as another building block to reinforce my identity. With an account I was also free to change up more money. No one asked questions as long as I wasn't changing more than $10,000 at a time.

From the apartment in Colorado Springs we started thinking about what we were going to do in the longer term. We liked the area: it was clean, the air was fresh and the climate meant snowy winters and warm summers. The views were spectacular. Colorado Springs was over a mile above sea level and the air was thinner and there were fewer bugs. It was rugged country and surrounded by mountains used for skiing and other winter sports. There were lakes where the fishing was good and a thriving hunting scene that I was keen to take advantage of. The people we met were friendly but they didn't pry. It felt like the kind of place where we could settle down and Debbie and I came to the decision that we would find somewhere more permanent.

I wanted to use some of my cash sensibly for the first time in my life. I couldn't work and had only been given limited funds and that meant I had to be careful. Renting was a waste of money. Property investment, on the other hand, made economic sense. Colorado was a desirable state. There was more going on there than in neighbouring Utah and Wyoming but it was still off the tourist trail. The skiing industry that arrived later in places such as Aspen and Wolf Creek was then still catering very much to the domestic market so we did not have to worry about running into too many Brits.

On my 'Places to live as a fugitive' checklist, privacy was top priority. Even in a small city like Colorado Springs I felt there were too many people and, in cities in general, people live too closely together. They were good places to get lost in temporarily, but not good to live in. Number two on the list was access to a community. I wanted to be somewhere connected, where there were people who would accept us but not ask too many questions. Number three was an escape route: we needed to live near a road or highway in case we needed to get away quickly. There was no point being too remote and we would have gone mad living somewhere isolated from the rest of the world. Number four was leisure. It was all very well having money to spend, but if I had nothing to spend it on, what would be the point of taking all that risk to begin with?

With all this in mind we began casting around to look for the ideal community in which to embed Mr and Mrs Stephen King. The car allowed us the freedom to start exploring the forests and mountains around Colorado Springs. It was beautiful country, full of majestic mountains and traditional old towns. We went further and further afield, exploring the mountains. We drove to the Ute Gorge and the Garden of the Gods, an amazing national park full of natural sandstone formations. We explored Pikes Peak, the highest mountain in the state. Eventually, 18 miles west of Colorado Springs, we hit on paradise. Woodland Park was high in the mountains above the cloud line. It had 300 days of sunshine a year, clean air and, when we moved in, only around 2,000 residents. There were no bugs or asthmatics because the air was too thin.

We found a four-bedroom house slightly away from the main town, with vaulted ceilings downstairs and quite a bit of land. We bought with cash and the transaction was easy. Every contact with England we could cut, we did. After a month in the US I knew nothing about the news back home – and, in

Woodland Park, neither did anyone else. UK news was never reported. The Securicor job might as well have taken place on the moon for all the relevance it had in our new home. It was one less thing to worry about. As long as I could keep up the lie and make people believe I was Stephen King, a photocopier salesman from Essex, I was safe. The main aim was to get settled somewhere. We did that. Then it was to work out how to make the most of the money, how to get Lee into school and, almost as importantly, to have a laugh. And we did.

CHAPTER 10

ACES HIGH

Midlife fugitive retirement didn't come easy. It takes planning to disappear from one life and start a new one somewhere else. First, you need money. Luckily we had that, but not as much as I would have liked. Second, you need discipline. You wouldn't believe how hard it is to cut yourself off from everything and everyone you know.

Back at home, Debbie and I both had family and one of the hardest parts of life on the run was knowing that we couldn't contact them. I had an elderly mother in London who wasn't in the best of health and I felt guilty all the time, knowing what my disappearance would have done to her.

Third, you need luck. Thankfully, we had plenty of that, mainly because the police back in the UK appeared to be inept. By the time we started settling down in Colorado, the investigation into the theft back in the UK was losing momentum and direction. I was unaware of this and continued to sleep with one eye open, waiting for the cops to burst in and take me back to Blighty. By all accounts, they realised early on that I had gone to the US because they traced Debbie's flight and knew she'd stayed in a hotel in Boston. The investigator in charge of the case asked if he could fly out and check out the lead but the request was refused. That was as far as they ever got.

They did have tip-offs from all over the world. According to reports, we were seen in France, Spain, Germany, Jamaica and Cyprus. The Cyprus sighting came in May 1993 and cops were so sure it was me their request to go and investigate was granted and a few of them went on a four-day expedition to check it out. It seems strange to me that although they knew Debbie was in the USA they weren't allowed to fly there and try to find her, but they were allowed to go to Cyprus. No wonder I managed to evade capture for so long!

While the cops were floundering and making my life easy, I started to work out the logistics of life on the run. Right from the start I realised that my change of identity meant that Debbie and Lee would also need new identities. Debbie's British passport was useless. She couldn't use her real name so I suggested one.

'You'll have to become Barbara King,' I explained.

'Barbie! You must be joking. I'll be Sarah.'

I wasn't going to argue with her. We became Stephen and Sarah.

I also realised Lee, who was three, would need to get into school if we were going to stay put. We placed him in a nursery, for which we only needed proof of address and we provided that in the form of mail. Lee got a place easily and the nursery fed into the elementary school system. Once he was in that he had a school record, after which there was no need for formal identity papers of any kind. He never missed any schooling and no one ever asked questions. The US school system was very fair at the time and the government believed that every kid had the right to a place. Even the children of illegal immigrants got a state education without too many questions or checks.

Getting Lee into the system was a weight off my mind. However, I was aware that there would be times when he would need a birth certificate so I started working out how to get a fake one. After a bit of research, I discovered that there were mail order certificate mills where anyone could purchase blank certificates and official grade blank paper. The sample documents came through with the word 'sample' stamped across them. There were catalogues full of different types of documentation and anyone could purchase them. In order to make a forgery, I had to work out how to get rid of the sample stamp and how to clone the design on a blank piece of official paper. It was the early days of home-printing technology and graphic software but I invested in the best on the market and taught myself the art of forgery.

US states are like countries and each has its own laws, governments and documentation. Each state had a design for birth certificates, some very simple, some more intricate. All

I had to do was find the most simplistic birth certificate and clone one for Lee. California's certificates were a joke – very basic. According to Lee's first US birth certificate, then, he was Lee King and he had been born in California. I was proud of my work. It looked completely genuine. There was an art to it. You had to scan signatures from one to the other. I took a degree of professional pride in my work and, 20 years later, I was gutted when my handiwork got seized by law enforcement and confiscated.

Where possible, though, I tried to avoid using the fake documents. There was no point taking unnecessary risks. I was never sure how joined up the different systems were in the US. Computer technology was still in its infancy and the internet was growing in popularity, although it was far from ubiquitous. Even so, I did not want to run the risk of being caught.

After the flight into Dallas I never used the Stephen King passport to fly again and only showed it once to get a driver's licence, when the official looked, made sure I was the person on the photo and that was it. I took a driving test in Colorado as if I was a new driver. I couldn't use my old UK licence and needed a new one in my new name so, despite having driven for decades, I took lessons so I could take a test with an examiner at the end of the course. I must have been the oldest learner in Colorado. I was in my 30s and the instructor was just a kid who realised I'd been driving for years and even commented that I'd been a car driver longer than he'd been alive. I passed the test first time and got a licence, which was really the only ID I needed. An official driving licence in the US was the main form of ID. It was the one universal document that everyone accepted. With a driving licence, opening bank accounts was easy and a bank account provided statements that could also be used as another form of ID. It was like piecing together a jigsaw. One document led to another and over time I started to build up a picture. The one issue I knew I would have to overcome in the long run was the lack of a green card, which allowed people to work in the US.

As I worked on building up the practical things we needed to reinforce our new identities, we never tried to adopt American accents and were always honest about being English. Debbie and I tried to get used to being Mr and Mrs King. It was hard remembering to call each other Sarah and Stephen and, early on in our adventure I realised that we needed a strategy to help us. While we always introduced ourselves as Stephen and Sarah to others, when we were talking to each other we used the term 'babe'. We both hated the word but it was easier than having to remember our false monikers and it became so common that we started using it in private as well. We didn't even discuss it. It just happened. We used it a couple of times and it stuck. It was an organic thing and it worked well because we were never caught out.

When we moved to our new home and as Lee started nursery inevitably we started to speak to people in the community. Woodland Park was a small town and people there were friendly. It was an expanding, up-and-coming area, which meant new faces were met with acceptance rather than suspicion. Most of the people there had come from somewhere else. People asked us where we were from in passing and out of politeness and we gave them the story we'd developed. Being an Englishman in America always got me attention but no one ever pried too much to begin with and no one questioned us. They accepted we were who we said we were. We made sure there was a balance of truth and lies in our story. People assume that to live the life of a fugitive I had to build an intricate backstory with loads of detail and nuance. But I didn't. I told people I had been a fireman in London. I told them I'd served in the army. On the whole I was honest about who we were, apart from our names and the fact that I was the UK's most wanted fugitive who had stolen a van with £1.2 million in it.

Establishing our ID as the Kings was one concern and the other was money. The cut I'd been given was not going to last forever and, at some point in the future, I was aware I would need to work. That was going to be hard without a bona fide green card. I needed to find a way of making the money I had stretch as far as it possibly could. The answer came during a weekend break. Colorado was the gateway to the western states and hopping on a plane to California, Nevada and Arizona was as easy as catching a bus. From the airport in Colorado Springs we were only a short, cheap flight from Las Vegas and one day I suggested to Debbie that we take a trip there. In the early 1990s Vegas was cleaning up the image it had of being a seedy desert town of casinos and brothels and was reinventing itself as a family destination. One of the new hotels, the MGM Grand, even had its own theme park. There was only one flight a week from the UK so it had yet to lure the British holidaymakers who flock there today. It was the ideal place for us to enjoy some family time and for me to indulge in one of my hobbies – cards.

It began innocently enough with a few hundred dollars. Back in the UK I had dabbled with blackjack and discovered I had a natural aptitude for it. The first time I played in Vegas I realised the knack had not deserted me. I soon doubled my money and I then walked away. The following night I went back to the casino floor and tried again. Once more I walked away with more money than when I'd started. I played with a bigger stake and kept winning. On the third night I sat at the table with a pile of chips in front of me when the pit boss walked past, noticed a couple of grands' worth of chips stacked up and comped me with food and drink.

In Vegas the house usually wins. If it doesn't, it will do everything it can to give itself the opportunity to win back in the future. So the practice of handing out free meals, drinks and accommodation to high rollers is commonplace. Most people think this is the casino's way of being nice to their regular customers. It's not, it's the casinos attempting to even out their losses.

The first time I stayed at the MGM Grand I walked away several thousand dollars in profit. In the process Debbie, Lee and me had been given loads of freebies. A month later I was back with more money and once again I won a considerable amount. The casino was keen to get me to return and offered us a complimentary suite the next time we were in town. A month later we flew back. From then on we went often and I more than doubled my money each time. I played blackjack and Texas hold 'em poker. I got hooked. One night I was playing and had completely lost sense of time. Debbie came down from the room and stomped over to me.

'Enough now, babe,' she said. 'It's 3.30 in the morning, are you going to come to bed?' She looked across the table and realised I was playing Mel Gibson.

In my youth I used to like playing cards and was always good at it. I joined the casino at the Grosvenor Hotel once and I used to play cards in the pub with my dad a lot. We played an old Irish game called 25s which was so complicated and weird it made blackjack seem very easy by comparison. There is no magic formula. If you follow the rules playing blackjack, you have a pretty good chance of making money. There is a degree of skill and strategy involved. I liked it because it wasn't a game you needed a great deal of luck to win at and I found the more I played, the better I got. I developed a sense for the cards and an instinct for the game. I got good at reading people and working out what sort of player an individual was. I knew who I could bluff and who was bluffing. I could read an opponent's body language and I'd know who was nervous and who was confident.

As the months rolled on we became regulars in Vegas and I expanded our pot of money, almost doubling it. I made it big enough to fund a decent standard of living. Our weekend trips became more frequent and we went at least twice a month. The added income gave us the extra cash to relax a little and start taking advantage of the leisure activities in and around our home.

We became particularly friendly with our neighbours, the Cox family and I was persuaded by the man of the house, Donny, to start bass fishing and hunting. I bought a small boat to go fishing and became involved in the local fishing club. After a year or so I joined the organising committee and became tournament director of the Pikes Peak bass fishing club. I travelled all over the country, towing the boat and entering bass-fishing tournaments. I bought Debbie a boat too, so she could play on the lake with me.

I started to make the most of the lifestyle. I'd always wanted to learn to fly and so I started taking lessons at a little airfield near Colorado Springs. I got to know the two guys who ran the control tower – actually a hut. One of them was a flight instructor and I offered to help out around the airfield in exchange for lessons. I drove the fuel truck and fuelled the planes.

It sounds extravagant but eventually I bought my own plane, a little Piper Warrior. It cost around $16,000 and I rented it back to the flying school who maintained and fuelled it for me. I also took my lessons in it, which were all free because it was my plane and I was doing unpaid work for the airfield management. It meant I could get a lot of air hours under my belt and I got my pilot's licence. I loved the freedom of flying around Colorado and the surrounding landscape. I forgot everything in that plane – there was just me, the clouds and the mountains. That was after my first solo flight, which scared the life out of me.

I flew to Kansas, which took a couple of hours and everything was going fine until I approached the airport I was scheduled to land at and only realised, as I came down, that the runway I was landing on had grass and plants growing through it. The tarmac was cracked, bumpy and broken and the plane bounced several times in bone jarring impacts. I taxied to the hangar, got out and walked into the airfield restaurant shaking, only to be told that I'd landed on the disused landing strip, rather than the nice new flat one which ran adjacent to it.

Debbie, who had been an air hostess but was scared of flying, came out with me once. As soon as the wheels got off the ground she started to panic. 'I don't like it, take us back,' she cried. I had to calmly explain that it didn't work like that and that we had to go up and come around before we could land again.

'No, no, take me back,' she panicked. We did one circuit and I had to land and drop her off.

I got the plane licence in Stephen King's name. It was easy enough then and there were no background checks. I applied, got a permit and a logbook and when the time came to take the test a guy from the government body that regulated flying came along and I went up with him. He watched me do my inspections on the plane, he checked my logbook and asked questions about flying but he did nothing to verify my ID. At the end of it I got a pilot's licence, another small piece of paper that folded up and went in my wallet.

Once I had my licence I regularly flew with Donny to

Nebraska, which is above Colorado. There was a hunting and fishing shop there that had its own landing strip. I used to go up there and do a bit of shopping. There was a lake and I did some fishing. I used the plane all the time. I'd go to the airport most days and if it wasn't being used I'd go up in it.

The flying community was a friendly bunch of people. I had several friends at the airstrip and I told them my story – that I was an English businessman and that I'd sold my company and was enjoying the benefits while I worked out what I wanted to do next with my life. As far as they were concerned I was a sort of Richard Branson figure.

We adapted to fit in with the locals. Woodland Park was in Teller County up in the mountains and because I'd been a fireman and knew about rescue and first-aid, I volunteered to be part of the Teller County search and rescue team. It was a voluntary band who mainly pulled lost and injured climbers and hikers off the mountain. I could have applied for the local fire brigade too because they were mostly volunteers but then I would have needed some form of background check and I could hardly put the London Fire Brigade down as a reference. On several occasions I went out with the search and rescue team and our endeavours made local news. Reporters came, interviewed some of the guys and took photographs. I would always stand at the back in line-ups and make sure my face was obscured by someone in front of me. We had regular training sessions and were also often in contact with the sheriff's department. While I was volunteering Debbie became involved with the nursery and school. She volunteered there as a helper. We were pillars of the community, two fugitives with a huge, dark secret, hiding in plain sight, enjoying a second chance at life.

CHAPTER 11

REV MAHER

hroughout our time in Colorado, Vegas remained a regular haunt. The MGM Grand, in its push to become a family resort, also offered a free babysitting service. Parents could put their children in clubs or with a registered minder for up to four hours. It was all part of the service, the acceptable face of gambling. There is an old saying: the family that plays together stays together. I'm not sure the playing in the phrase means slots and poker though.

I looked on the Vegas trips primarily as business. They were work. The tables in MGM Grand were my office and I played cards to boost our family retirement fund rather than for fun. But while we were in town we made sure we took advantage of the leisure opportunities. We ate out all the time, which was affordable even when we weren't enjoying complimentary meals. Most of the casinos ran ridiculously cheap all-you-can-eat buffets. They lost money on the food but provided it cheaply as a way of luring punters to the gaming floor. We joined queues of overweight holidaymakers lined up for cheap ribs in the windowless, clockless interior of countless casinos. It was a surreal world and I could see how people get trapped in it, chasing losses until they lose everything.

One day I was at a table playing Texas hold 'em and there was just me and a young American guy left in the game. Everyone else had folded. He was about $20,000 down and I could tell he had nothing. But he was still trying to make his money back, hoping that I'd lose my bottle before he did. I could have wiped the floor with him. His fiancée was at his side. They'd started the night in a bubbly mood, were clearly enjoying a break away together. But their evening had turned sour. Vegas did that to people. Eventually I 'saw' him, I could have carried on but I wanted to put him out of his misery and stem his loses. I saved him from himself and took his money. The look of devastation on his face made me realise that Vegas wins in the end and I made a pact with myself that, after I'd doubled my money, I'd stop going.

But before I did I had some traditional Vegas business to attend to. Debbie and I got married in one of the chapels that the city is famous for. We chose a traditional one, rather than an Elvis-themed or drive-thru chapel. The motivation was twofold. Firstly, despite appearances, I'm a romantic at heart and I loved Debbie and wanted to make it official. Secondly, a wedding certificate provided another solid piece of documentation to reinforce our identities. We booked Lee in to the kindergarten in the MGM Grand theme park, hired a car to take us to the chapel, which supplied witnesses, and we got married. We officially became Mr and Mrs King (the fact we did it under false identities caused a lot of legal debate many years later when no one could decide whether we were married or not because, although we married in a legal ceremony and had a legal licence, we gave false names). After the wedding, I went back gambling – after all you have to earn a living don't you? We returned home with a marriage certificate and wedding photographs that we proudly framed and put on the wall.

On the surface, life was great. I had money and I was enjoying myself. Anyone looking in from the outside would have envied our lifestyle. I appeared to be the epitome of a self-made man. I was a pillar of the community, a community rescuer, a pilot and a competitive fisherman. We had a lovely home, a happy son, we had friends and a decent social life. But people didn't really know us as well as they thought they did. Questions that pried too closely into our past life in the UK were subtly deflected and we never got into deep conversations with anyone. We kept everyone at arm's length.

Despite my outward cheery disposition, I was still constantly in fear of capture. I spent my life looking over my shoulder, expecting that at any moment the game would be up. The months went on and turned into years and with the passing time the gaps between the paranoia got longer but something would always happen that would fill me with fear and anxiety.

Someone would mention something to do with the police or joke about robbing a bank and I'd wonder if they knew. A police car would go past and I'd have palpitations. The sound of an English accent was enough to bring me out in a cold sweat and one of the reasons Vegas became less of a draw was because more Brits started going there.

Debbie and I never talked about our worries because, as far as I was concerned, there was no point adding to the low-level anxiety that we both knew we had to accept to live the life we had chosen. We knew the door back to the UK was closed. The plan was to get by and become a normal American family. I knew that at some point the money would run out and that I would have to work in some capacity and this still presented me with a real challenge. While I had money to live on and time to spare I needed to build up solid profiles through documentation for all of us. I became obsessed with documentation and identities.

Getting Lee ID was hard because he was so young. Through research I learned that as he got older I'd be able to build up his identity and establish himself as a citizen. His fake birth certificate would allow him to get a driving licence. The driving licence was the root from which everything branched out. With his birth certificate – which was good enough to fool most government officials – I was also able to apply for a social security card for him. You could apply at any age but it didn't look so odd if you applied when children were young. I got him a legitimate social security number so, when he was older, he would be able to go and get work.

There was one big ID no-no for Lee that troubled me. There was no way I could get a passport for him. For that he needed a genuine birth certificate, one that could be traced back to a birth record in a state ledger. It might well have been the case that the passport office only did spot checks on records but I could never take the gamble. I had to assume that if I applied for a passport for my son, his birth certificate would be scrutinised. A certificate without an official record would raise suspicion. So, it was never an option. It would have been easier to apply for an English passport for him because we still had his British birth certificate but, again, I couldn't be sure how linked up the systems were in the UK and whether the passport application office was linked to the police. I took calculated risks and exercised caution and knew that at some point in the future I was going to have the very difficult task of explaining to Lee that he couldn't ever have a passport and could never travel abroad.

For Debbie and me, I considered all the different types of ID that would allow us to work. There were different options. Non-citizens were allowed social security cards but they had the words 'Not suitable for work' printed across them. A green card was for resident aliens and entitled the holder to work and live in the US with the same rights and privileges as a citizen. Generally, you got a green card for four years and after four years you became a citizen if you stayed out of trouble.

There was a market in fake social security numbers and green cards, mainly because of the demand from Mexicans who came across the border and worked illegally. Many of them bought and used documents from legal immigrants and, while we probably could have gone down to the border and bought one, it wouldn't have suited us. Employers would soon have become suspicious when a pair of Brits presented IDs in the names of Juan and Juanita Valdez.

Instead, I went into the realms of the extreme. I discovered that in the US a baptismal certificate sufficed in certain circumstances instead of a birth certificate. The USA was and still is a religious country that places God and the church above government. Church documentation carried as much weight as government documentation. It all stemmed from history. Church and state were independent and the state had to accept the church's documentation. It was still a young country and when the travellers forged out into the wild west where there were no institutions and little governance, they didn't have birth certificates but they did get baptised so that became proof of identity. Consequently, many states still endowed baptism certificates with the same authority as a birth certificates.

I discovered there were lots of places where a God-fearing man or woman, drawn to religion, could sign up to ministries online or through mail order, fill in a form, do a multiple-choice exam, pay a fee and become a clergyman. They could then officially baptise people and, most importantly, issue their own baptism certificates, which is why, a couple of years after settling in Colorado I found my calling with the online ministry, the Church of the New Light or some such crap, and became a reverend.

I got a certificate and, for a fee, could order blank baptism certificates that I used in place of birth certificates to apply for other IDs for us. And at the same time, I continued to trawl the certificate mills for other documents, which included social security cards and college degrees. Technically they were illegal and were supposed to have the word 'sample' written across them, but some didn't. And with my printing and cloning expertise, I managed to build up a nice library of varied documents. I was lucky to be over there in the golden age when you could do that sort of stuff. It was easy to find. You could buy magazines in shops that advertised books about making your own ID. I bought state seals and all sorts of things. It was a nice little hobby, much more interesting than stamp collecting.

But despite my efforts and master forgery, I knew that it didn't matter how much documentation was attached to Stephen King: he would never be able to get a proper job. He was a fake Brit who would never be able to work, which meant that when the money ran out, I'd either have to take low-paid, under-the-counter work or I'd have to become someone else and put Mr King into retirement, which would then have all sorts of implications for the rest of the family. Being a fugitive was not easy.

Luckily for me, years before I came to the USA my brother Mick had lived there, married an American woman and had a green card. It dawned on me that at some stage I might have to steal that ID because he still had the legal right to live and work in America. It was the nuclear option because there was every chance that doing so would set alarm bells ringing somewhere, but it was an option, nonetheless, should things get financially sticky.

And they did. After a happy year in Woodland Park, in which the price of our house had risen, I realised that the pot was depleting a bit too quickly and it was time to cash out of the high life – literally. Most of our money was tied in the house, the boats and the plane, which I knew at some stage would all have to go. They were investments. To free up funds and maintain the standard of living that we were enjoying we put the house on the market and bought land down on the plains below the mountains where it was a lot cheaper. The step down was not as dramatic as it sounds because we bought a lot of land – 80 acres in all – and had a sectional house built on it, which was still a big place. We were on farmland and we had a 500-foot well sunk and a septic tank dug. We paid to have power connected. That was how it worked over there. You didn't have to worry about planning permission. If you needed water you dug a well and if you needed power, you paid for the poles.

Life didn't have to change and the pressure was off for a while as our coffers were replenished. We only moved down the mountain about four miles and we didn't change our social circle or Lee's school. I was still in the search and rescue. I still went hunting and fishing and flying. I also started doing some cash work for friends because I had a computer and the software. The Cox family owned a motor mechanic shop and I did the software for their invoicing.

I went hunting regularly with Donny and I bought a rifle

and a handgun. We hunted elk and, permitted to shoot one animal a year, we donated the meat. We'd camp out in the mountains, sit round the campfire and have a few beers. It was proper cowboy stuff. One day we were in our campsite when a gang of Mexicans rode through on horseback with guns shouldered, chasing something they'd seen. They had all been drinking. I flagged them down and remonstrated with them. I was holding a rifle at the time and had my pistol on my hip. The Mexicans argued back and things became tense – this was a real-life Mexican stand-off. They eventually went but returned in the evening with the intention of continuing the argument. Me and the friends I was with were sitting around the campfire and we all had our guns to hand. Things could have got nasty but common sense prevailed and we talked to them and calmed them down.

Every state had its own rules about guns and there were two main types. There were concealed-carry and open-carry states. Colorado was an open-carry sate, which meant you could walk down the street with a gun on your hip if you didn't go in a school or a bank. The laws were contradictory – you could go to one state and would have to display your handgun on the seat of your car where a cop could see it, then drive into another state where it had to be in the glove compartment. In Colorado, if you had a gun on your hip or carried a rifle down the street you were fine. But if you hid it inside your clothing then it was a concealed weapon and that was illegal. The sight of so many guns on display took a bit of getting used to but after a time it just seemed normal.

Every so often we talked about the UK. I missed some food, such as curry; there were no Indian restaurants in Colorado. I missed public transport – you couldn't just jump on a train over there. Everyone drove. The people were a lot friendlier but at the same time there was a big thing about giving people personal space that I hadn't found in the UK. If I got within two foot of someone they would often ask me to back off.

We had to learn new rules but none of them were hard. I had to learn new sports because sports were a focal part of every school and parents were expected to get involved with coaching. Football was soccer and it was a girls' game. Rugby was non-existent. I had to learn the rules of baseball, hockey and American football but I drew the line at basketball because it was too much like netball. I loved the games because they were really good. I ended up coaching.

We stayed in Colorado for two and half years. We never got any indication the that the police were after us. In the UK, there had been a BBC *Crimewatch* reconstruction and appeal but the case had gone cold. The news cycle had moved on. I was the UK's most wanted man but, ironically, was technically working for the cops in the US because the sheriff's department oversaw the search and rescue team I volunteered with. Sometimes I wondered what would happen if someone did discover our secret. Part of me liked to believe that we would have been safe because Americans love bandits. Look at their heroes; Bonny and Clyde, Al Capone, Billy the Kid. They were all crooks. Americans root for the underdog, especially the anti-establishment figures.

The hardest thing about disappearing was breaking contact with family. We never got the opportunity to say any good-byes. We were there one day, gone the next and I tortured myself thinking about what it must have done to my mum. When I left, she was very ill. She'd survived cancer and had her pancreas removed five years before and her health was in decline. I knew it must have been awful for her to lose me and Lee, who she doted on.

One day about a year into my exile, I couldn't stand it any longer and, for the first time, I went to a call box and I dialled her number. When she answered, I couldn't speak for a few seconds. My heart was in my mouth.

'Mum?' I whispered.

'Oh, my God! Eddie? Is that you?' She sounded distant.

'Yes, Mum, it's me.' I could hear her crying. 'I'm so sorry, Mum. I just needed to call you. I can't say where we are but we are safe and we are happy.'

She sighed. 'Thank you, son,' she said. 'Now I can die in peace.'

'I love you, Mum.' I was choked with emotion. I hung up and stood there for ages. I needed to know how she was and I wanted to put her mind at rest. I knew it would probably would be the last time I ever spoke to her. It was. She died several years later, while I was still on the run.

CHAPTER 12

TAKING
THE MICHAEL

The problem with becoming part of a community is that people get to know you and the more they get to know you, the more questions they ask. After two and a half years of good living in Colorado the questions began to get more pointed.

'Why don't your family ever come and visit?'

'Why don't you ever go back to the UK?'

'Why don't you ever talk about your family?'

We had answers for each question but it was uncomfortable all the same.

'We don't have much to do with our family in the UK. We lived there all our lives, we don't need to go back, we've seen everything there is to see there.'

You might not believe this but I didn't like lying. Plus, I wasn't very good at it. I really liked the people we had made friends with, particularly the Coxes, who had taken us under their wing when we first moved to Woodland Park. I felt bad having to lie to them. Who knows, perhaps if I told them the truth they'd be fine and wouldn't grass. I couldn't take the risk though so all relationships had to be superficial to a degree.

There were even a few times when someone questioned my fake name. 'Stephen King? Like the author? That's a made-up name, surely.' On more than one occasion I found myself cursing the goons who thought it was a good idea to send me into exile with the same name as the man who wrote *Rita Hayworth and the Shawshank Redemption* and *The Green Mile*, two of the most popular stories about prisons every written.

The longer we stayed, the more people knew us and the more links we had. I had networks of friends at the airfield, in the fishing club, at Lee's school and in the search and rescue team. We weren't forthcoming and were a bit vague and they began to get suspicious. It didn't help being an Englishman living in America because people wanted to know about life in the UK. I just wanted to forget it.

I started to get an uneasy feeling about things. It felt like my luck was beginning to run out. I was also concerned about money. Even though we'd freed up funds by moving, a year later they were running low again. Something was going to have to give and sadly the next sacrifice was the airplane, which pained me considerably. I started making inquiries around the airfield to see if anyone wanted to buy it off me. That in itself caused a few raised eyebrows and a bit of small-town gossip.

Inside the troubled world of Fast Eddie Mayhem

Pub fire bombing link with Securicor robbery

STOLEN: Space Cruiser used to transfer money   EMPTY: Home Maher shared with his girlfriend   MISSING: Eddie Maher

---

Police quiz mystery lover in the life of Fast Eddie

By JOHN TWOMEY
and BOB McGOWAN

THE mystery lover of missing Securicor guard Eddie Maher is to be quizzed by detectives hunting the daring thief who stole £1.3 million.

Maher vanished last Friday with the money from his van. His regular girlfriend Debbie Brett is believed to have joined him.

Now detectives hope the mistress left high and dry by "Fast Eddie" will provide vital clues about his disappearance.

Maher's two-timing was uncovered after officers double-checked intelligence files.

They are convinced exfireman Maher, 37, carried out the daring raid with the help of major criminals.

They are looking for at least two other men in connection with the theft.

Accomplice

Maher vanished as a colleague was making a cash delivery to a branch of Lloyds Bank in Felixstowe, Suffolk.

The two-tonne

MISSING: Two-timing Eddie Maher

the robbery, was later dumped. Police first thought Maher, of South Woodham Ferrers in Essex, may have been forced to take part in the crime after Ms Brett was kidnapped.

They now believe he was a willing partner.

Former 999 operator Debbie, 27, and her three-year-old son Lee

EMPTY: The Essex house Eddie shared with Debbie and her son

They think Maher, Ms Brett and the boy may now be abroad.

One possible hiding place is America. The couple recently enjoyed a dream holiday in Florida.

Flash

Publican Brian Covington, who took over the Gardeners Arms in

he did. He used to drive a Jaguar XJS when he ran the pub but he did not seem especially flash with money or ambitious.

"He just was not the sort of man who wanted a champagne lifestyle. He was more at home with a pint of bitter."

Mr Covington revealed it was Nottingham-born Debbie who got fed up

MISSING: Live-in love Debbie Brett

with all the locals — they never had a bad word to say about him.

"The Gardeners Arms was his first pub and they ran it for about seven months."

Maher, a one-time gasfitter, joined Securicor last year after he was invalided out of the fire service.

Reward

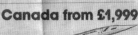

Canada from £1,999

The press lapped up my story and were intrigued by my 'troubled world'… © *Daily Express*

'WE'VE HAD SUCH A LOT OF APPLICANTS FOR THE VACANCY!'

"Go on admit it — you don't trust me, do you?"

...it was only a matter of time before my story was lapped up by the satirists too.

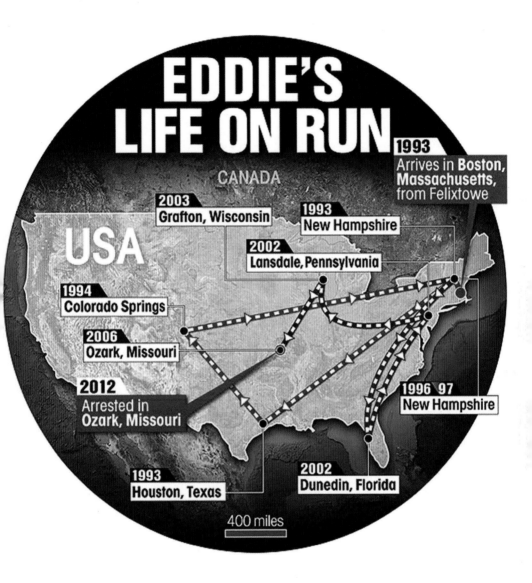

EDDIE'S LIFE ON RUN

CANADA

USA

1993
Arrives in **Boston, Massachusetts,** from Felixtowe

2003
Grafton, Wisconsin

1993
New Hampshire

2002
Lansdale, Pennsylvania

1994
Colorado Springs

2006
Ozark, Missouri

2012
Arrested in
Ozark, Missouri

1996 97
New Hampshire

1993
Houston, Texas

2002
Dunedin, Florida

400 miles

My life on the run began when I arrived in the USA in 1993 and lasted for nearly 20 years. I kept moving on as frequently as I could – settling my family all over the country, from New Hampshire in the north to Florida in the south.

Above: It must have been tough on little Lee when his parents decided to up-sticks and flee to the USA. He didn't know a thing for so long but it was only a matter of time before he began to ask questions. Here we are before the event that changed our lives – in Templemore, Ireland.

Below: The new Mr and Mrs King! Debbie and I tied the knot in Vegas in 1994, marrying under false names and causing a subsequent legal headache for the US authorities. On the surface life in Colorado was great – but soon it was time to move on again.

Life in the USA was totally different to my life back in the UK: fitting in was tricky at first but then it became second nature. I learnt to ice fish in New Hampshire (*top*) and hunt in Colorado (*bottom*). I became just another American living the dream.

The quality of life was pretty good in the USA and I enjoyed staying in some wonderful places, including New Hampshire (*top-left*) and Colorado (*right*). I was also awarded a pilot's licence – something I would have never expected when I living back in east London only a few years before. I even bought a plane (*bottom*)!

Nielsen Media Research Service Awards

After working as a trucker during the early years of my time in USA, I began a career at media company Nielsen. I started off as a TV repairman but soon moved up the ranks. It wasn't long before the FBI managed to tracked me down, however, and after a stint in jail in the USA I was extradited back to Britain.

FUGITIVE FAST EDDIE IN UK ON £1.2M THEFT RAP

By HARRY HAWKINS

A SECURITY guard on the run for 19 years after £1.2million was stolen from his Securicor van was extradited to Britain yesterday.

Eddie Maher, 57, was escorted by FBI agents as

Maher . . . cop mugshot

he was flown from Chicago to Heathrow.

The fugitive – dubbed Fast Eddie – was handed over to Suffolk Police officers who formally arrested him on suspicion of stealing the money.

Cops have hunted Maher since he vanished in January 1993, along with the cash he was supposed to be delivering to banks.

He was arrested in February in Ozark, Missouri – where he is thought to have lived under a false name – after a tip-off.

Yesterday he was driven 100 miles to Ipswich, where magistrates remanded him in custody. Maher did not enter a plea at the six-minute hearing.

He disappeared from outside Lloyds bank in Felixstowe, Suffolk, while a colleague was inside making a delivery. His

van was abandoned nearby, and cops believe 50 bags of cash were loaded into a stolen Toyota.

Maher's rented home in South Woodham Ferrers, Essex, was found empty. His partner Debbie Brett and son, three, had flown to the US the day before.

In court yesterday, Maher was told he would be committed to crown court on July 24. He said "Thank you" before being led away. *h.hawkins@the-sun.co.uk*

Returning to the UK was difficult for my family and me. We're still feeling the effects of our lives on the run.

Eventually one of the blokes who I knew there offered to buy it. He was one of the more suspicious acquaintances I had. He never fully bought into my semi-retired-photocopier-tycoon spiel and had always been quietly sceptical. I was wary of him and when he offered to pay in four instalments I should have run a mile but there were not any other interested parties and it was much better for me to sell privately to someone I knew. He was good for his word for the first instalment but when the time came for the second payment he raised an eyebrow.

'I think there's something shady about you, Steve,' he said.

'What are you talking about?' I replied.

'You've come over from England. No one knows you. You have all this money and buy planes and boats. We never see any family apart from Sarah and Lee. You don't have any other friends apart from the ones you made when you moved here. It's like you've got no past. I think there's something shady about you. Maybe I'll speak to the cops.'

They say it takes one to know one and he was a thief. His instincts were right, of course, but I was impotent. Apart from decking him, there was nothing I could do except laugh off his suggestions and reiterate to him that he owed me money. The weeks went on and he never paid up. Whenever I asked he replied with the same smug answer.

'I think you're dodgy. Why don't we speak to the cops, see if the plane was bought legitimately?' And by not doing anything about it, he knew I was hiding something. He even voiced his thoughts to other people at the airfield, telling them, 'I reckon Steve's wanted, what do you think?'

That was the straw that broke the camel's back. It was time to go. People gossiped and talked in a small community and I knew it wouldn't be long before the tide of goodwill and friendship we were riding would turn. I learned over the years on the run that there is a timeframe involved in fugitive living. At best you get three years somewhere before the suspicions and questions start. People you've spent lot of time with begin to realise there is something strange about you because they still only know as much about you as they did at the beginning.

When the rest of the money for the plane wasn't forthcoming I sold the boats. I explained to Debbie that we were going to have to move. We didn't quite have a fire sale but it was clear to outsiders that we were clearing house. The combination of diminishing funds and neighbourhood suspicion were forcing us away. I sugar-coated it for Debbie. 'We'll be able to free up some money and see another part of America,' I explained. But she had the same feelings I did and was finding the questions about our lack of history and wider family and friends uncomfortable.

We put the house we'd built on the market and told friends that we were going back to England for work. They had realised that the money was running out anyway so it reinforced our story. We didn't want to move and were both upset about leaving Colorado – I could have stayed there for good, given the opportunity – but we tried to look on the bright side and sat down with a useful web resource called Sperling's Best Places to find a town in which to begin again.

I was anxious to put a bit of distance between us and

Colorado for several reasons. Firstly, the further we went, the less likely we would be to run into people we knew from Colorado. Secondly, we wanted to see a different part of America and experience a different climate. We chose New Hampshire because we had been there when we went on our US holiday several years before. We knew it was a decent place. We had always wanted to live there and it probably would have been our first choice. However, early on after my little transgression, we had decided against going there because it was on the east coast which had more connections with the UK and Europe. After several years away and with no indication that I was being pursued by Suffolk constabulary's finest I deemed it a safe place.

The house sold for a profit, which freed up some more funds and we slunk out of Colorado and drove all the way to New Hampshire to start another new life. It was like leaving the UK. We couldn't tell anyone we knew where we were going and lied about forwarding addresses and numbers. 'We'll drop you a line with our new details,' I lied. I never saw or spoke to any of them again.

I was aware by that point that I would need to start working in the very near future. We weren't living hand to mouth but the money wouldn't last forever. Even with careful budgeting I reckoned we only had a year. In the US, if you don't work you don't earn and if you don't earn you don't live. It was very simple. Even if you sign on for unemployment you only get help if you have worked in the first place and we never had. I needed an official green card, not a forged one. And I needed one that was attached to a real individual, not to Stephen King. That meant we would all have to change identities and I'd have to start from scratch with forging and cloning.

I arrived in New Hampshire as Stephen King and we took a short-term rent on an apartment while I looked for somewhere to buy. We found a house in a picturesque lakeside town called Laconia, a smaller place than before; we were downsizing with each move. I paid for it outright then, a few months later, I mortgaged it to get a lump sum of cash we could live off. It was not a great way to manage finances because we were making mortgage payments from the lump sum. However, desperate times called for desperate measures and I didn't plan on ever paying the mortgage off. I needed to give myself some breathing space and the scheme worked nicely for a year until it was time to finally put Stephen King into retirement and get a job.

The only way to get my green card was to steal my own brother's identity, which sounds dramatic but was easy. I knew his date of birth so all I had to do was write in and say I'd lost my green card. They sent me a new one. It even had his picture on it. Luckily, I looked like him. The green card meant that I then had the freedom to work, which was a huge weight off my mind. I applied for a driver's licence and became Michael Maher. It was as easy as that to gain a new identity, but problematic in many other ways because it meant we had to move once more. In Laconia, I was Stephen King to all the neighbours.

So we had been in our lakeside home for a year before we

packed up, took Lee out of his school and moved. I didn't bother selling the house, I just left it to be reclaimed by the mortgage company and then sold again. Don't feel too sorry for them, though – the mortgage was for somewhere about 70 per cent of the total value of the property, so they would have made a nice profit when they sold at market rate. The difference between the money owed on the mortgage and the penalty for cashing it in early technically belonged to Stephen King, who sadly was not available to collect.

We liked New Hampshire so we decided to stay. The state motto was 'Live free or die' and New Hampshirites were very big on individual liberties and against big government. It was my kind of place. I liked the sentiment, especially if that meant living free from jail. It was a winter state and the fall – or autumn as it's called in the UK – was amazing. People came from all over the world to see the foliage. The large lakes meant that there was plenty of fishing and there was hunting in the mountains and woods.

We moved from Laconia to the capital, Concord, which was only one city down-state. We had kept ourselves to ourselves in Laconia because I was always aware that at some point I'd have to change identity so we didn't get to know many people or get involved in the community. I doubt our overnight disappearance registered with anyone and for that reason it seemed safe enough to move nearby.

Concord was bigger than Laconia but not as picturesque – it was more of a functional town. Michael Maher and his family moved there in 1996. I was hoping that by reactivating my brother's US identity I would not inadvertently assume any problems he may have had when he lived in the US but, thankfully, it seemed he had behaved himself. Assuming his identity was risky but I didn't have any other options if I wanted to work and earn enough money to raise a family. In hindsight it seems crazy that I was able to live as my own brother without inviting any scrutiny from law enforcement agencies, particularly given that UK police had a solid lead in the US. They knew Debbie had flown there and then disappeared. They even knew she'd flown into Boston, which was in New England, the region where we were living. But that was three and half years before and the trail had gone cold. The US police were not looking for me, they couldn't have cared less about a crime that happened several years previously on the other side of the world. In the mid-1990s, international law enforcement was not joined up. Nowadays an alarm would be ringing somewhere.

When I got Michael's ID I assume a piece of data went through a system somewhere but only in the USA – the UK obviously wasn't joined up. Even if the two were linked in some way, it was not a priority for the FBI. There was a statute of limitations for theft in the USA which, at the time, I think was four years. In the USA I would be home and dry by 1997 when any case brought there would be dropped and I would no longer be prosecuted.

It was a relief to change from Stephen to Mick because I was able to work but it took several months to get used to. I would sometimes get called Mick and not realise the person talking to me was addressing me. I got into the habit of not answering people and telling them I was hard of hearing. Lee was old enough to realise that people were calling me by a different name so I explained to him that Michael was my middle name and people were using that. He was six and at that age kids will believe anything. If they can believe in Santa, they can believe in name changes.

We rented an apartment in Concord and, for the first time since I hastily left my Securicor job, I started to look at ways to look after the family. With the last few thousand dollars we had left I took a commercial driver's licence (CDL) course, which was the US equivalent of an HGV licence. I'd driven engines in the fire brigade so I knew my way around big vehicles and the CDL would be a good back-up plan because everything in the US moved by road. There was always work for truckers and it was the kind of industry that attracted people who kept themselves to themselves and didn't ask many questions.

I passed the CDL test and was allowed to drive the big rigs. The first job I had was driving the magazine truck for a firm called Green Mountain Explosives, which was really cool. I did the local runs to quarries around New England and inevitably I travelled on my own because nobody wanted to come with me. The main cargo was ammonium nitrate soaked in diesel, the same compound people used in fertiliser bombs. In the side of the trucks there were lock boxes that held all the detonators and the caps. They had to be kept separate from the main cargo. In essence, I was driving around a truck bomb. I carried hundreds of bags of explosives and, when I reached the drop-off, the explosives were unloaded and packed into large drilled holes in whatever rock face it was that was being blown to smithereens that day. The ammonium nitrate would be primed with something like a stick of dynamite to get the party going and then the whole thing would be electronically detonated from a safe distance. The people at the quarries taught me how to do it a few times. I parked several hundred metres away from the blast site and the crew would retreat back to the truck and I'd blow the horn for them to do the blasting. It was magic, it was like being back at school.

With a job and security, our lifestyle changed. We were comfortable and settled down to regular life again. We were a normal working family without debt. We started to lay down roots, I started coaching Little League baseball and we became friendly with a couple who had a place on a nearby lake where we went most weekends. We used the same back story we had used in Colorado: I was a British businessman who had sold a company, made some money and was now working again. It was silly to keep making up new stories. Debbie was still Sarah but she was now Sarah Maher rather than King.

In 1997, while we were in New Hampshire, my son Mark was born. He was planned. I had always wanted a family, although I never wanted more than two and never wanted any girls so it worked out just right. When Debbie fell pregnant we were living a more settled family life and were not looking over our shoulders quite so much. We also realised that having a child in the US would be no bad thing if the British police ever did find us. Surely the Americans would be more inclined to look favourably on us if we had a son who was a US citizen? Extradition might be a bit harder. It wasn't the reason we decided to have another child, but I could see the advantages. My job also came with a medical plan that covered family so Debbie's appointments were taken care of.

We were becoming more and more American. Lee spoke with an American accent and never asked about the UK and his other family and we had a son who was a fully fledged American citizen, born and bred in the US of A. The fear of capture was still a niggling annoyance and reared its head every so often but the UK, Securicor, Suffolk police and my criminal past were getting further and further away.

CHAPTER 13

KEEP ON TRUCKIN'

Mark's birth in the USA provided us with another much-loved son and it also provided me with another much-loved bona fide form of ID that I used as a template to carefully clone and create a new birth certificate for Lee.

Onto this document I printed the revised names of his mum and dad. I didn't tell him about it and as far as he knew he was still Lee King. He was Lee King in the school system and to change his surname would have invited unwanted questions. It suited the situation to have two birth certificates, one in the name of King and the other in the name of Maher but, as far as the US authorities were concerned, he was Lee King and that's what he remained. It was complicated and I knew it would get even more complicated as Lee got older. He would inevitably ask questions and I couldn't help feeling that there were issues being stored up for the future. I wasn't the only one – unknown to me, several years after my disappearance, one of the cops in charge gave an interview and, in one of the only smart insights the old bill ever had into my circumstances, said that while I might be able to keep off the radar indefinitely, one day my son would crop up and give my whereabouts away. But more of that later.

We were actually trapped in the USA. I could do a lot of clever things with software and a printer but the one document I could never forge was a passport. None of us had one. We could never cross a US border, even to Canada or Alaska. I wondered how likely it would be for Mark to get a passport when he was older. Luckily, we had everything we needed there. The USA was not a bad place to be a fugitive. My fugitive father checklist goes something like this: safe place to live, employment options, low-level government interference, free society, leisure activities, variety. When we wanted a holiday, the options were limitless. I learned to ski and we took Mark and Lee. For someone like me who liked gambling, there was always Vegas. For boating, there were lakes everywhere. Like the ocean? There was the Pacific, the Atlantic and the Gulf of Mexico. Fishing? Sailing? It's all there. Then we had all the forests, every landscape we could ever want to visit.

In the USA in general and in New Hampshire in particular, there was a big anti-surveillance culture. Americans were dead set against any government prying and any new forms of technology that allowed the government and government agencies to keep tabs on citizens. For example, they would never use facial recognition cameras and they even suspended speed cameras because, in US law, anyone accused of a crime has the right to face their accuser in court and you can't face a camera.

For us, each move had been a step down from where we started, as the money gradually reduced and by the time we got to Concord, it had all been frittered away. The retirement was over. We were no longer living lavishly but each time I had a few dollars spare we went over to Vegas or took the kids down to Disney in Florida. I was happy to be working and the Michael Maher ID didn't appear to have attracted any unwanted attention.

After several months blasting the landscape with the explosives company I was called into the office one day for a chat with my manager. 'We like your attitude, Michael,' he said. 'You've got a real aptitude for the technical and safety side of things and we'd like to train you up to be a blaster. There will be a raise in your salary level in accordance.' He was smiling.

'Interested?'

'Er, yeah, that's really good,' I answered.

The next day I went in and reluctantly handed in my notice, giving them some cock-and-bull story about moving on to a new job somewhere else. Annoyingly, to handle explosives I had to be licensed and to get a licence I would have had to undergo several security and background checks that would have caused all sorts of problems. I started looking around for another job immediately and, over the next months did a range of different things, none of which were particularly exciting or interesting. Digging irrigation ditches was a low point.

I eventually got a job for a company called M&S Trucking and became an owner/driver. At interview I explained that I had experience driving heavy vehicles and formerly drove fire engines. I didn't mention my spell as a Securicor driver.

The firm did lease-purchase arrangements. They organised the finances so drivers could own their own trucks and then work for the firm as contactors. The system allowed drivers the freedom to be self-employed and also to take on other jobs with other haulage firms, which made a lot of sense logistically because trucking was all about planning routes and picking up loads. A successful run could take me away for several weeks all over the country delivering scores of different consignments for several different customers. For example, from New Hampshire I would be given a job to drive a container to South Carolina. Once I delivered that I would look for other jobs and maybe get a run from South Carolina to Dallas. In Dallas I'd find another job that might take me to San Diego on the west coast. From San Diego I would then start looking for jobs that would take me back across country, possibly to Chicago. The idea was get back as close to New Hampshire as possible because all the time I was carrying a load, I was earning money. The average rate was a dollar a mile and I would sometimes be out for five weeks driving 500 miles a day – 50 mph for ten hours. There was no end of work because every single commodity and all goods in all homes in the US were carried on a truck at some point. The country is so vast that if you were a trucker prepared to put in the hours you could earn a good living. I was a drop-and-hook driver, which meant I never had to load the cargo, I just picked up the container and took it.

My truck – or rig, to use the common parlance – was fitted with all the mod cons a knight of the road needed to sustain a life on the highway in the late 1990s. Behind the driver's cab there was a living area comprising a bunk, some cupboard space and a TV. Most importantly, up front there was a CB radio. In the days before ubiquitous mobile phone ownership, CB radio was the trucker's best friend. The airwaves were alive with blokes who had watched *Smokey and the Bandit* too many times. Everyone had their own call sign. Truckers didn't have much of a sense of humour so most of them had names they hoped made them sound macho – Eagle Wheels, Road Runner, Chrome Cowboy, that sort of thing. They all spoke with same Texan cowboy drawl that evaporated when you actually met them in person and realised they were from places like Philadelphia and Detroit. I learned the lingo of the road. Cops were 'bears', '10-4' was okay, '10-20' was location, 'eyeball' was a face-to-face meeting. I chose my call sign. It was Language Barrier and was apt because no one understood my accent.

I started off with small runs and stayed out for a week or so at a time but soon extended my runs because the work was always available. I went down to the Mexican border and up to the Canadian border but had to limit my runs because of the passport problem. I had to stipulate to the firm I worked for that I didn't want to go into Canada or Mexico. Fortunately, all drivers could stipulate places they didn't want to go. There were several other drivers who also refused cross-border runs so it didn't arouse suspicion. The bosses understood about Mexico because a lot of lorries got hijacked there. It was harder to explain Canada but they knew I had a green card rather than a passport and I explained to them that it was harder for me to go back and forward across a border than it would be for an American citizen with an American passport. They didn't like their loads tied up at the border for ages while drivers got their paperwork stamped so they understood. Another common no-go was New York City because very few drivers wanted to negotiate an 18-wheeler in the city streets. There were enough people who would do it and enough consignments elsewhere in the country to keep me busy. I carried all kinds of cargo, including hazardous materials and chemicals but unless there was a dangerous load, mainly I didn't know what was hooked to the back of my truck. It was usually an unmarked shipping container.

When I first started they tried to put me in a partnership with another driver. Legally, after ten hours on the road you had to stop and sleep. You'd be mad to try and do any more than that anyway because you'd pass out with boredom. The driving speeds and distances were monitored by tachographs in the trucks which recorded everything on paper disks which drivers were required to hand in. The idea of putting teams on the road was to overcome the ten-hour limit. One driver would sleep while the other drove and then they would swap.

Theoretically, if you had enough provisions and didn't need the toilet, two of you could stay out on the road for weeks, just stopping for fuel. The quicker you did a run, the more runs you could fit in and the more money you'd get. I didn't get to choose my road-buddy and, unfortunately, the bloke they put me with was as nutty as a fruitcake. The final straw came when I woke up one day after a few hours of sleep in the back of the truck, poked my head through the curtain that divided the sleeping quarters from the driver's cab and realised we were in the middle of a white-out snow storm, barrelling along at 30 mph, 20 feet from the truck in front of us. I could barely see anything apart from the tail lights.

'What the hell are you doing?' I screamed. 'You're going to get us killed!'

'It's what you do in blizzards,' he grinned. 'We all keep to the same speed and no one stops. There are eight of us in a line following the doors of the one in front.'

'What happens if the one in front crashes?' I shouted.

'We all crash,' he cackled.

'This is insane. Park up and wait for the storm to pass,' I begged.

Eventually, he went on the CB and told the other drivers in the suicide express that his co-driver was chicken-shit and that he was pulling over at the next stop. After that I chose to go out on my own and be the captain of my own ship. My luck had held well for several years; I didn't want my flight from justice to end in the bottom of an icy ravine because of some gurning fake cowboy.

The CDL was a good investment and gave me something I could always fall back on wherever we were and whatever we were doing. With a CDL I knew I would always be able to get a job of some description in an industry that didn't ask too many questions, even if it wasn't a top earner. It was perhaps one of the few times in my life where I looked to the future and did something that made financial sense.

On long-haul runs I slept in the truck. I had a TV and later I had a phone in it. In the evening I would pull into a truck stop and, once I was parked up, I would run a lead into the cab for electricity. The stops all had clean showers and restaurants. They were amazing places; some of them were like mini-resorts and could accommodate over 500 trucks. The big ones in the hotter states had portable air conditioning lines you could run into your cab to keep you cool at night.

While the facilities were good, the company was disappointing. Truckers were horrible people. They were all oddballs. Personal hygiene wasn't high up on their list of priorities. The stops all had showers but they didn't get used very often.

I criss-crossed the whole of the country. Texas was the worst state because it was just a huge great empty space. It took two days to cross it and, overall, it was featureless. There wasn't anything pretty to look at so I just trundled across with my speed restricted to 50 mph. I dared not go any faster because Texas cops were hot on enforcing speed limits. It was boring, dead time. I drove from truck stop to truck stop listening to the radio. In Texas it was easy to doze off behind the wheel. It happened quite a lot on all the highways.

The two most eventful things that happened to me in Texas were getting a speeding ticket and witnessing an accident. I paid the ticket straight away and once you paid up, that was it, there were no repercussions. I got another ticket in Pennsylvania after driving across a bridge up to the toll booth and being momentarily distracted by a fire by the side of the bridge. I didn't reduce my speed fast enough and got hauled over by a patrol car. When I said there was a fire by the road, the cop explained it was from a gas plant. I disputed that ticket and was confident enough with my ID to go to court to argue against it. Everyone was encouraged to fight speeding tickets. I ended up getting a reduced fine because the courts plea-bargain everything and do deals with people to move the process along quicker.

The accident concerned an 18-wheeler that went over on its side. I came across it and stopped, went over and dragged the driver out of his cab. He had already reported it on the CB and I happened to get there before the police. I made sure he was comfortable and when the cops came they asked what happened. I told them that I didn't know and that it was just luck that I was passing. When the ambulance came and the cops started to talking to paramedics I made my excuses and left.

Like many of the other drivers I tried to drive through the night and sleep through the day because there was less traffic. As I got paid by the mile and not by the hour, time spent stuck in traffic cost me money. But the night work, long hours and inactivity all added up to an unhealthy lifestyle. I think having a heart attack was probably the leading cause of death for truckers.

At one stage, the industry did acknowledge that there were a lot of issues around loneliness and isolation so they started a campaign to get couples to partner up and drive as teams but it was not a very family-orientated way of life and, even if you did go out together, one of you would be asleep while the other was driving. I took Lee with me on one trip and he wanted me to drop him back home after a few hundred miles. Every time we went past something interesting he wanted to stop and look at it but I couldn't because I had a delivery to make. He soon got fed up.

Other problems included hijacking, which was particularly prevalent in the north-western states. I heard stories of drivers who had parked up at night leaving their engines running to provide heat and power. While they were asleep robbers put gas in the air intake, knocked them out and robbed their loads.

As far as I was concerned, while trucking provided me with much-needed money, I hated it. I could just about handle the driving but the long weeks spent away from my wife and kids really took a toll. It was a horrible life for someone with a young family. Mark was just a baby and I was seeing less and less of him. It was no fun for Debbie, either, being left on her own. Sometimes it felt like I was away forever. I tried to balance it out and do two weeks away and then one or two weeks back home but there was so much work and the jobs took me so far that it always ended up being four weeks at a time. It would be common to get stranded somewhere waiting for a few days for the right job to bring me back in the right direction. By the time I'd completed two or three deliveries, two weeks had gone and I was at the other end of the country.

I lasted a year before I decided that enough was enough and quit long-haul driving to go back to driving for local companies. I started working for a chicken processing company and drove down to Virginia where the chicken farmers prepared the chicken. I drove a big refrigerated rig and hauled chicken pieces up the eastern seaboard.

It was only ever a stop-gap and I saved enough money to take an information and computer science course and got an associate degree in computing. I'd always had an interest in technology because of the forgery and cloning and thought that perhaps I could turn it to a more legitimate purpose.

CHAPTER 14

RESPECTABLE ME

As the fifth anniversary of my hasty exit from the shores of the UK came and went, it almost became believable to think that I'd got away with it. In the US the statute of limitations had passed. I wasn't sure if that meant I couldn't be arrested by American cops or not and I didn't want to go and get legal advice about it, for obvious reasons.

We had steered clear of all UK news and as far as I knew everyone in Britain had forgotten us. The USA was our home, our kids were American and we avoided Brits. The hardest part of it all remained cutting ourselves off from family and friends. I often wondered about Mum. I tried not to think too hard about it because when I did I had to face the awful realisation that she might well have died and, if she had, it meant I wasn't there for her at the end. I never said a proper goodbye and I wasn't at her funeral. It was too painful to contemplate so I buried my head in the sand. The only contact I had with the UK in all the time was that one call.

In hindsight I think my brothers and sisters probably understood. We came from the kind of family that weren't great respecters of the law and, like a lot people, I'm sure their attitude would have been 'Good luck to you'.

Debbie struggled with the enforced exile too. She missed not being able to contact her family and I felt bad all the time about the situation I'd put her in. It was a strange sort of limbo we were both in. We were prisoners in paradise. With my green card I had the ability to control our destiny to a degree and to get a job and work but we could never have passports and we could never leave the US. And the fear that one day I would be caught never completely left me. I was always looking over my shoulder and some days I'd have a feeling of dread and wake up thinking, Today's the day, this is when I get nabbed, but those days were few and far between with the passing of time. Before I'd changed my name to Michael Maher, when the money was running out and people were starting to ask awkward questions, I had a few moments of doubt and even thought that maybe it would be better for everyone if I just handed myself in and faced the music. But then I thought about jail and I thought, Nah.

Back in the UK, on the fifth anniversary of the heist, the cops did their best to try and revive a bit of interest in the case and released new information to the public that they hoped would pique their curiosity and lead to some new developments. The cops confirmed that Debbie had travelled to Boston the day before the money disappeared. The details had been known for years and loads of news reports rightly speculated that I had gone to the US but, for some reason, the police chose not to confirm them. Half a decade later they thought this information would give the case renewed impetus. They even released the name of the hotel Debbie stayed in. The national media, by all accounts, were unimpressed and the only paper interested was one of the locals in East Anglia, which sent a reporter to Boston to ask a bemused hotelier about a guest who had stayed for a night five years previously. A similar press release had been drafted back in 1995 and that had also confirmed that police believed I was in the US. But that earlier notice never got issued and sat on a hard drive on a police computer somewhere. It did seem sometimes that the police were making things very easy for me.

Ironically, at the same time that the police were trying to get people interested in the story again by telling people there was a Boston link, I was working in Boston. If they'd have bothered getting off their arses and investigating, they might even have found me. After all, I was living under my brother's identity at a registered address and it wouldn't have been too hard. I probably even passed the reporter who got sent out there while he was investigating the story. Boston is a small city and the offices I was based in were only two miles from the hotel Debbie had booked into on her first night away. I sometimes passed it.

Being British had certain advantages in America. People

tended to look at me in a different light when they heard my accent. Brits were more trustworthy and authoritative. Even my cockney accent sounded refined to American ears. It was always a bonus in job interviews, which was why I never struggled to find work.

After trucking and spending time moving between jobs, I began looking for something that would allow me to settle and even start a career. I saw a newspaper advert for a job with a company called Nielsen that was undergoing a large expansion programme across the whole of the country and was looking for people with technical experience. The job involved going into people's homes and fitting their television sets, videos and other equipment with monitoring devices. Applicants had to be trustworthy and law-abiding so I was perfect. It was based in Boston, Massachusetts, the next state down from New Hampshire and commutable in 90 minutes from Concord. I applied and got an interview during which I was asked to complete a set of practical and technical tests along with what I called the anti-idiot tests – basic general knowledge tests to make sure applicants could spell their names and tie their shoelaces. I got the job.

Nielsen was a big media company which operated globally. It supplied ratings data for television shows and channels and for the media industry in general. Nielsen's TV systems monitored what people were watching and when they were watching it. It was state-of-the-art and people had to be specially invited to become part of the Nielsen ratings survey, as the network was called.

The company chose households that fulfilled certain demographic criteria. They had to be representative of the average for the area they were in. So, for example, if the census said that the average Milwaukee household was white, professional, earned $35,000 a year, had two children aged 6 and 12 and the man of the house played golf, Nielsen reps would find households that matched the criteria and ask them if they wouldn't mind having their viewing habits monitored.

Once the equipment was installed, Nielsen statisticians used the data gleaned from it to project viewer numbers for specific channels and they would also be able to say what type of people were watching which shows in which locations. The system was called an 'area probability market'. It was complex and the data was then sold on to advertisers and television companies and used to set rates for different channels, time slots and for specific shows. Because the data was used to set commercial rates it had to be faultless and completely independent, which meant that Nielsen was unable to pay anyone to host its equipment and to be monitored. They had to do it voluntarily. Nielsen hit on a very clever marketing technique. It created a brand which bestowed status on people. You had to be invited to be a Nielsen rating home and, if you were invited you were part of a very special club; you represented thousands of other people. The ploy worked. People clamoured to be part of the Nielsen rating system.

My role within the whole process was to install the monitoring devices in people's homes. It was a technically demanding job because the equipment was soldered directly in to anything that took a signal for TV viewing – which, back then, meant video cassette recorders, TVs and cable set-top boxes. Every device in a household would have to be connected. There was no standard set-up procedure because devices were all made by different manufacturers and the insides of each were different. Installers carried around piles of technical manuals for all the big manufacturers. The job involved connecting wires to specific points in the circuitry and then running the wires back to a central unit that would then be connected to the phone line to send data. I would routinely have to open up the back of televisions and solder equipment. It was intricate work. Then I had to run wires out and if I smoked anything I had to replace it.

I was part of a team who were operating in and around New England, expanding the network to take in more houses. The company made a fortune and was very well thought of. It was a good job. Employees were well looked after. There was a family health plan, a pension scheme and the social life was good too. The hours were favourable and I got to see plenty of my family. It was idyllic. I had a career and, because the company had offices nationwide and was expanding, there was plenty of scope for progression. The company actively encouraged employees to stay and climb the career ladder. I enjoyed the work. I liked the technical side of it and I liked being my own boss to a degree, working on my own and meeting new people.

At home Mark started school and Lee excelled at baseball

and American football. I continued to help out coaching with the teams. There were always Little League reports in the local papers accompanied by photographs. Mark and Lee appeared in the press several times and, if you look hard enough on some of the old sports reports in local Concord newspapers, you'll see photographs of me, skulking in the background, trying to keep out of shot. I tried to keep a low profile but it was hard when I was part of a small community and had sons who were good at sports. We were a normal American family just like all the others. We kept our heads down, worked hard and tried to blend in. Only Debbie's and my accents marked us apart.

I toyed with the idea of trying to create more IDs for Debbie in a different name but knew it would be too risky. Over the years the internet had grown exponentially. Through my work and my interest in computers and systems I was very aware that developments in IT had linked more and more public systems. Documents were also evolving to become increasingly complex and harder to forge. They had watermarks and holograms and chips embedded in them. The golden age of home forgery was dead.

We lived several uneventful years in New Hampshire as a regular family without arousing any suspicions. And then, one morning in 2001, while I was driving to work, something momentous happened that would affect the whole of the world and impact on our situation as well. It was 11 September and, as thousands of people were also on their way to work, a bunch of lunatic fanatics flew two planes into the Twin Towers, one into the Pentagon and one that crashed in Pennsylvania. It was a horrendous act of terrorism which killed almost 3,000 people. It was the most devastating attack on American soil since the assault on Pearl Harbor and left the country reeling. In the weeks, months and years after, America and Americans changed.

Everyone remembers where they were that morning when the tragedy began to unfold. I was driving from Concord to Boston, on one of the smaller roads that headed south towards New York. I was by the state border when I saw cars pull over at the side of the road and others turning around and heading back north. I was listening to music but I had a work mobile phone and, as I was wondering what was going on, Debbie called. She was close to tears. 'Something's happened in New York,' she said. 'A plane has crashed into one of the buildings there. It is terrible. One of the towers is on fire. They are warning people to stay away. I don't know if you should go in. They are advising people to stay away from Boston too. It is awful Eddie, there are people trapped in the building. They are telling people not to travel if they don't have to and to stay away from the cities.'

It was obvious from the warnings that the crash was more than just a terrible accident and I followed the advice and turned around to drive home. I switched the radio on and listened to the coverage. I heard the shock on the announcer's voice when the second plane went in. My heart was in my mouth. The whole nation was in a state of panic and shock.

I got home and Debbie was in tears. We hugged and watched the news.

When the towers came down I thought of all those firefighters and emergency workers who lost their lives. We had friends who worked in New York and, although we didn't lose anyone close, we did know families who lost members. Every community along the eastern seaboard was affected. One of our friends lost a brother.

In the weeks that followed it seemed as though a deep depression fell over the whole country. The USA was in collective mourning and everyone was in shock. The country had always seemed invincible. The nation as a whole believed it was impregnable and looked at events abroad with detachment. Americans believed they were 100 per cent safe on home soil and that, although they were targets abroad, they were protected in the USA itself; the nation would never get hit. The scale of the attack left people scared, vulnerable and numb. Then, after a while, the shock started to give way to anger and defiance. The country came together, people supported each other. There were Stars and Stripes everywhere. In New England in particular, people did everything they could to show support and solidarity. It was hard not to get swept up in it. So many firemen died and I had always seen myself as a fireman; I associated with them. In the aftermath the New York fire brigade was crying out for help and for new recruits. I would have loved to have applied and to have helped but I couldn't.

Gradually, life got back to some form of normal but it

was never the same. Ground Zero became a focal point for the national mourning. I went there to pay my respects. And things started to change after 9/11, almost imperceptibly. People became a little warier of foreigners of any description. It didn't affect us too much because we were already embedded in the community – and even we started getting more suspicious of outsiders. A lot of the friendliness went out of the USA that day. The nation as a whole started to close ranks and the government and federal agencies seized the opportunity and, under the auspices of homeland security, put in place a series of security measures and clampdowns that directly affected the civil liberties that Americans held so dear. The nation accepted them all because it felt scared and exposed.

Agencies became more joined up. Domestic travel in America became harder. The government founded the Transportation Security Administration (TSA), an agency of the Department of Homeland Security that held authority over the security of the travelling public. It came in very quickly. Travel documents were now required. Domestic flights became more like international flights. We needed a passport for ID purposes, where a driver's licence had sufficed before. Security at all transport hubs was beefed up. Queues were horrendous and it became a chore to travel. Police officers were more vigilant and wary of strangers; they had more power and they did more racial profiling. CCTV and surveillance were increased throughout the country.

Before 9/11 a lot of people from different countries had

travelled to the US to gain their pilot's licence because it was cheap and fairly easy to organise. Now investigators looked at all foreign nationals who had obtained flying licences in the country. At some point they would have come across my record. Fortunately, it was in the name of Stephen King so no one knocked on my door.

The implications for anyone with a dubious identity were serious. I realised that all the measures being rolled out would make it a lot more likely that I would get caught. They were not looking for me, I was confident of that after so many years, but the increased scrutiny made it harder to fly under the radar. Debbie's driver's licence also ran out – all US licences needed to be renewed every three years. After 9/11 we couldn't get it renewed because we didn't want to take a chance. I'd been lucky enough to adopt Michael's identity but there was nothing we could do for Debbie, which meant, in effect, she didn't exist in the USA. She couldn't work legally and she wanted to work. I joked and called her the longest stay-at-home-mum in history. She didn't see the funny side. In the end, to earn money, I applied for homeworking type jobs for her where it didn't really matter who did the work as long as it got done. We did paper rounds out of the car. It was good money. From that time forward everything also had to be in my name, which Debbie found hard. It was another friction point between us but, thankfully, she is a very forgiving person.

It became harder to go away because we couldn't simply fly to Vegas or down to the Gulf. Even the railway operator

Amtrak instituted ID checks for a time so we had to drive anywhere we wanted to go.

It wasn't long after 9/11 that we finally left New England. We'd been there for five years and, as had happened in Colorado, I got an uncomfortable feeling that we had outstayed our welcome. People started asking the same old questions, particularly after 9/11. 'Why don't you talk about family?' 'Haven't you got any friends from before you moved here?' 'Why doesn't anyone from the UK come and visit you?' 'Why don't you ever go back to visit?' We fobbed people off with vague answers and that made them become even more inquisitive. It got to the point where people stated to speculate about our mysterious past.

'I've got it,' exclaimed a friend. 'You're in the witness protection scheme, aren't you?' It was a joke but it resonated. I realised that people were starting to think a little too hard about us. The witness protection scheme accusation repeated itself several times over the following years when we moved to different parts of the USA and it was always my cue for another move.

I had been thinking about doing another flit several months before the opportunity to move up in Nielsen presented itself and it couldn't have come at a better time. There was a promotion on offer that would mean relocating to South Carolina. We'd have to make new friends, find new schools for the kids and rent a new home but it would also give us a convenient, legitimate excuse to go somewhere new where people didn't know us and wouldn't ask so many questions.

I applied for the position and got it. Within a few weeks we packed up our stuff, said goodbye to our friends and headed off. It was pattern that would repeat itself for the next 12 years.

CHAPTER 15

AVERAGE JOE

When Mark was 4 and Lee was 12 we moved to a town called Anderson in South Carolina. By now I was a career man in a decent middle-ranking technical role with a large US corporation. South Carolina was off the tourist track. There were hardly any British people there. It had some beautiful beaches, busy seafront resorts and majestic state parks but it didn't have the draw of nearby Florida, which attracted the UK visitors and as a result I didn't hear a UK accent all the time I was working there. It was as good a place as any in the USA for a British fugitive to hide out, not that I saw myself as a fugitive now. I'd pretty much swallowed the lie that we were an all-American, regular family. I suppose I was in denial: if I continually thought about the reality underneath the façade, I would have gone crazy with anxiety. If you tell yourself a lie enough times, you believe it eventually and, although every so often something would happen that reminded me that I was on the run, my day-to-day life was as average as everyone else's. I had the same work stresses, the same worries about paying the bills and raising a family. I tended to think more about those problems than the likelihood that the cops would be knocking on my door.

Anderson was a decent city in which to live. It called itself the friendliest city in South Carolina and was a typical southern state. It was clean and the people there were pleasant enough but they were not as nice as those we'd known in New Hampshire. We'd never lived in the south before so it took some getting used to. Without being unkind, many of the natives were what you might call a bit strange – some would say backwards. A lot of people lived in trailers. It wasn't a rich state. They are also very proud of their Confederate history, which comes with lots of questions over slavery and civil rights.

My job involved a fair amount of travel to some of the more remote areas outside of the cities and the folks could be quite eccentric, living in remote communities and in their trailers in the middle of nowhere. I came across some really strange things up in the mountains. On one job I was installing equipment in a trailer and I needed to run some cable from one end to another. The easiest way to do it was to run the cabling under the trailer, rather than start drilling holes through the walls. The trailers were raised and had cladding and mesh skirts around the bottoms of the outside that could be easily removed to allow access underneath.

On the day in question I removed a panel and crawled into the cavity underneath. It was boiling hot and full of stale, still air. I crawled to the far end of the structure towards the cable that I'd poked down through a hole in the floor above. As I was reaching up to pull enough of the wiring through, my leg slipped down into a hole to my left. I looked down instinctively to see what I'd fallen into and saw a pit. In the bottom of it I could make out the coiled bodies of snakes. I don't think I've ever moved so fast. I screamed. I pushed myself up and cracked my head on the trailer above me. I scrambled out of the cavity and refused to go back until someone had come in to remove the reptiles and make the area safe. The owner was nonplussed and couldn't understand my safety worries.

'It's just a snake pit,' he shrugged. 'We have them all over the place here. They'll only bite you if they feel threatened.'

On another job I started to crawl under a trailer and heard hissing. In the gloom at the back I saw a pair of eyes staring at me and realised there was a family of wild cats living under there. It stank. I backed out carefully. From what I could make out there was a mother there with her cubs.

Nielsen remained a good company to work for and they looked after their employees. They laid on several social events a year and one of the treats for the team I was assigned to was a rafting trip through one of South Carolina's forests. As we were travelling through the countryside, the guide mentioned that the location was where the 1970s' movie *Deliverance* was filmed. With its cast of inbred red-necks the film had done little to bolster the image of the rural southern states. While

I never encountered any forest-dwelling, male rapists on my travels, I did sometimes drive into villages nervously humming the film's famous theme tune, 'Duelling Banjos'.

Perhaps I'm not being too fair to South Carolina. It did have its advantages but for us it felt very different to the other places we'd lived. Debbie, in particular, had a hard time there. There was a degree of casual racism that she found hard to cope with and it did feel like the people were wary of outsiders. We didn't make many friends and found it hard to settle. She hated the wildlife there too, the way we would go into the garden and get covered in fire ants.

After less than a year we both decided that it wasn't the place for us. I was unhappy with the work I was doing anyway; there are only so many dodgy backwoods a cockney can take, so I asked my bosses for a transfer and was offered another posting within the company at their head office and call centre in a place called Dunedin in Florida. Initially, I was wary. Florida was where the vast majority of Brits went. Dunedin was on the Gulf coast near Tampa and had beaches and islands that visitors flocked to. However, a bit of research told me it was off the main tourist trail and well away from Orlando and the big theme park resorts. We looked up trusty Sperlings and Dunedin rated highly. It looked like it was worth a punt. The climate was excellent, the crime rate was low and it was right on the coast. There was plenty of fishing and golf (which I'd become hooked on) and there were good schools for the kids. Debbie couldn't wait to get out of Anderson and so, in the end, it wasn't a hard decision. I stocked up on long-sleeved shirts to cover my tattoos and grew a moustache so I looked like a proper American – it lasted a couple of weeks, as far as I remember.

Just ten months after moving to South Carolina we packed up our belongings once more and moved to the sunshine state where we rented a house. The job was different and another step up in the company hierarchy. I was in tech support so I was based in the office and advised technicians on the road who were having problems. I was a troubleshooter for the workers around the country. I had to interview for the job but by that time I had been with Nielsen for several years and it was a shoo-in. I didn't have to show ID. The interviewer asked questions about being British and life in the UK, probably to make sure I was going to stay in the job. I would fob them off. 'I don't go back,' I said. 'I'm more American now than I am British. I have no family over there. I've seen everything there so there is nothing to go back for any more. My kids are American and I'm committed to the American way of life, yessiree!' I only ever had to provide one reference from the UK when I started with Nielsen. I forged that and never needed another because all my references came from my previous superiors in the company.

As my new job was based in the office and not out on the road I got to know my co-workers better than I had before. There was a thriving social life and the people were friendly and welcoming. Inevitably, I drew a bit more attention than most of the other newbies because I was a Brit but in Florida they were used to the English accent so Debbie and I didn't get the sort of reaction we had in South Carolina where we stuck out.

Our house was on the Gulf coast, right by the beach, which was perfect. It was also right by a golf course so I got to indulge my hobby while Debbie took the kids to the seaside. It was warm, laidback, I was earning decent money and there were parrots living in the trees. Life was all right.

Our next door neighbour was the former mayor of the town and was hilarious. He was a real character and his claim to fame was that he kept the Scientologists out of Dunedin. The main Scientologist town in the US was next to us in the south, Clearwater. The mayor told us they'd initially tried to buy up land and settle in Dunedin but he kept stifling their planning applications and vetoing the sales of land until they gave up. We still saw plenty of them around, though. They bought up a load of motels along the coast in which they'd house their new recruits while they brainwashed them and convinced them that sooner or later the mothership was coming back to reclaim their alien souls or whatever baloney it was that they believed. We'd see them wandering with their hands painted purple (apparently it was some sort of purification ritual). They wore different coloured clothes according to their level in the organisation. Debbie started working for a housecleaning business, having become friendly with the owner, who paid in cash. She went along with the owner once to price up a job at Kirsty Alley's house, one of the actresses in the comedy *Cheers*, who happened to be a Scientologist.

The activities in Florida were very much centred around

the ocean. There were lots of marinas and boat clubs and I joined one. I didn't have the funds to buy a boat but the club owned its own and allowed members to take them out. About a mile or so off the coast there was a national park called Honeymoon Island, which was joined to the mainland by a causeway. It was a nice day out by boat from Dunedin because you could get there in 20 minutes, pitch up, have a picnic and enjoy the sea. There was a specific route we had to take to get to it by water because there was a big sandbank to negotiate. Zooming back one day – possibly after a couple of cold beers, I can't remember exactly – with Debbie, Mark and Lee, I went off the channel and ended up on the sandbank. The boat beached and plopped over on its side. We ended up having to get out and pull it out with a rope. Debbie was wary of getting in a boat with me again after that.

Boating mishaps aside, the kids loved living on the coast. They both swam with wild dolphins one day. They were out in the bay and initially crapped themselves because they saw a group of fins coming towards them and thought they were sharks. Then something leapt out the water and they realised it was a pod of dolphins.

Florida turned out to be a great place for the family. We took advantage of all it had to offer. Despite my natural aversion to touristy places we went to the Disney World resort and to Busch Gardens, another popular theme park. We went off season but Disney World still had too many English people in it for my liking. It was a bit nervy in the Magic Kingdom. We'd taken Lee there when we first moved over and he was young. At that time, news of my escapade was still fairly fresh and if people looked at us for too long we tended to turn and walk the other way. We never queued up. We used the fast-track system, which was very new at the time and it meant there was only ever about six people in a queue for any ride so less chance we'd be stuck waiting with other Brits and less opportunity to chat. That said, my dislike of Brits was not just the result of my criminal situation, but that the English abroad also tended to be obnoxious.

The only downside of Florida was hurricane season. We got hit by tropical storms three years in a row. Our windows blew in one day and several trees on the golf course came down. There was no power afterwards, which meant no air con.

We stayed in Florida for two years and would have stayed longer but for a work opportunity that I couldn't miss. I was climbing up the corporate ladder and another promotion was presented. It was a hard choice. Debbie would have stayed in Florida forever if we had the choice but I wanted to provide a better life for my family by honest means and in the end I accepted the promotion, based in Philadelphia. We hadn't been in Florida long enough for anyone to get suspicious or start asking questions this time; the move was purely professional.

The kids understood we needed to move because of my work and they hadn't got established, although it was hard for Lee because he was in the football team and was enjoying it. It helped that many professional people in the US moved around for work. We met many people in the same position and, generally, if you worked for a national company and got promoted, you were expected to relocate.

So off we went to the city of brotherly love – Philadelphia. The less said about it the better. It was a shithole. After Florida it was like being sent back in time fifty years. It was a ghetto. The whole city was a pit. It was the capital of the USA at one stage and there were two blocks in the middle that were the historic centre and they were nice but the rest was awful. I decided to drive the family into the city one day for a look around. I expected it to be like most big cities and to have dodgy parts on the outskirts and then gradually improve as we approached the centre and property prices increased. We drove further and further in and I was thinking, when do we leave the ghetto area? In Philly, it never ended. There were people standing on street corners, huddling around burning braziers. We didn't dare pull off the main drag. We stopped at lights and people clustered around the car, trying to sell stuff through the window. I turned around and drove out, vowing never to drive back in again.

Thankfully, we lived outside the city but even there it felt uncomfortable. The people were really abrupt. They seemed to see right through me and, on several occasions, I was questioned vigorously about my past and asked outright if I was wanted. There was no social subtlety.

I was promoted to senior rep when my manager moved and, shortly after, a position came up at his new location for a supervisor in Green Bay, Wisconsin. I put in for that and, thankfully, got it, which allowed me to move the family out of Philly. It was a much nicer environment on the banks of Lake Michigan. In 2006, we moved again and spent time in a place called Grafton just outside Milwaukee. By that time we'd managed to stay out of trouble and had been on the run for almost 14 years without a whiff of law enforcement apart from two speeding violations. But then Lee, who was 16 and of school-leaving age, decided to embark on a period of teenage rebellion. I couldn't tell him what the implications were but I did impress on him that the last thing I needed was to have the cops sniffing around. To begin with he got involved in some stupid juvenile things, not even as bad as the things I'd been doing when I was his age. He got busted for being in state parks after curfew with groups of mates. It was just messing around but we weren't in a position to deal with attention. We couldn't have people looking at us and that was when we started to get worried. My concerns must have seemed disproportionate to Lee and he started to question me. He was not stupid: all those questions that other people had asked over the years about our complete disconnect from the UK had started to play on his mind. He started asking questions about his family in England. What about his grandparents? His aunts and uncles? Why didn't he know them? Why didn't we have photos of them on the mantelpiece?

I couldn't tell him the full truth but I didn't want to lie completely so I told him he had an older brother in England. Lee wanted to contact and meet him. I told him I didn't have his details; following an acrimonious divorce, Terry had remained on his mum's side. But he still wanted to meet him.

I told him he couldn't. He had also realised he didn't have a passport. He went through a stage where he wanted to join the army and I told him he couldn't because I worried there would be security checks.

At the same time, he met a girl, Kayla and they got very serious very quickly. Within a short space of time Kayla got pregnant. It seemed that history was repeating itself. Lee was adamant he wanted to move out and move in with her and start a family. We did all we could to make him graduate from high school but once he'd left he didn't want to go to college or university and he rented an apartment with Kayla. As soon as he left school he was gone. It was a tough period. Lee was starting to realise that something wasn't quite right with the happy family façade we had built around him and his brother. He knew there was something there under the surface and, quite rightly, he wanted to know what it was.

Lee and Kayla had a daughter late in 2007. He called her Sophie and Debbie helped them out and took care of her. But when she was still very young, Lee and Kayla split up. It was acrimonious. Around the same time I was offered another promotion in a place called Minneapolis St Paul in the neighbouring state of Minnesota. I wanted to protect Mark and Debbie and put some distance between us and Lee, who I felt was a grenade at the time and was going blow up and take us all with him. It was a very hard decision to make. Lee was still only young but he was causing too much trouble. The prediction made by that policeman years before, that I'd be given away by my son, seemed pretty astute.

CHAPTER 16

EVERYTHING UNRAVELS

L ee is my son and I love him, which is why I'm not going to go into loads of detail about his private life. That's his business and this is my story. But I will say that after Kayla, he embarked on a series of disastrous relationships. Lee would be the first to admit that in his late teens and early 20s he was unlucky in love. That's putting it mildly. He beats himself up about the mistakes he made all the time so I don't have to. He has to live with it and at the time we tried to support him.

Debbie, Mark and I moved up to Minneapolis St Paul where I continued to rise up the corporate ladder. Most towns in the USA give themselves little subtitles, such as 'friendliest town' or 'happiest town' – Minneapolis St Paul called itself 'the most liveable city in America'. I wasn't sure what exactly that meant but it was as pleasant as any and fairly anonymous and average, which I liked.

Moving had become a way of life and, although subsequent reports like to speculate that our constant moves were the result of a life on the run, evading capture at every turn, the truth was less exciting. Most of the later moves were the result of promotions and work commitments. Of course they would have helped had I been on the US police radar but, remarkably, the US police were never looking for me. Theoretically, I could have lived in the same place under my own name and, if no one ever grassed or no one ever googled, I would have been untroubled by the law. There were only one or two occasions when I sought a move because I was concerned by people asking too many questions – in Minneapolis St Paul, 15 years after the heist, I met another person who became suspicious.

He was my boss at work and over the months he started to get a little inquisitive. The worst person a British fugitive could possibly meet was an anglophile – someone who loved the UK and wanted more than anything to go there. Unfortunately, that's just what my boss was. He would have been happy talking all day about the UK. He followed British news and he wanted to hear all about what the UK was like. When I wasn't forthcoming he got frustrated and then he got suspicious. He wanted me to recommend places he could go and when he started thinking about booking, he started asking me for contacts of people he could meet who could show him around. He wanted names and numbers. This went on for several months until, fortunately, he retired. With his position vacant

I saw an opportunity to take a big career step forward and I applied for his job and got it. It was a big jump which put me in charge of two states, Wisconsin and Missouri, and involved a lot of travelling. I was finally a corporate suit. I was senior management in one of the most respected media companies in USA. I'd done it all on a false identification while on the run from UK police. I know I shouldn't be proud but, let's face it, it was quite an impressive achievement. I must have been one of the best-paid and highly regarded fugitives on the planet.

Life was good but good things never last and with the position came the threat of foreign travel. Nielsen was an expanding company and was always on the lookout for new markets in other countries. It also held annual conferences and events for senior staff that sometimes took place abroad so I was constantly anxious, worrying that I would be called upon to go abroad somewhere.

While I was a corporate face in a respectable position in the heart of a blue-chip company, my eldest son on the other hand was living a life almost identical to the one I'd escaped from.

Lee's problems wouldn't have been an issue for an American family or for anyone who wasn't in the situation I was in. We could have probably resolved them a lot easier had I not been on the run. But as it was we just had to avoid him because anything that drew attention to me would have implications for Debbie and Mark. In hindsight, I think a lot of his problems resulted from his desire to know about his history in England and my unwillingness to tell him. Until that point he had been a regular US kid who went to school and high school and played football and baseball. But when I saw him making all those mistakes in his relationships I saw history repeating itself. He didn't have contact with Sophie after he split from Kayla and that upset Debbie, who had been close to her granddaughter.

I think by that time in our journey, Debbie and I were finally getting tired of the constant change. We wanted to settle down somewhere and when Nielsen got bought out and underwent a restructure that would involve a relocation to Chicago I finally said, 'No, we're staying put.' Mark was in high school and doing well. None of us had particularly enjoyed our time in Philadelphia and, even though Chicago was supposed to be a nicer place, I didn't want to live in another big city. I was also aware that at some point I would be required to travel further afield and knew that would open a whole can of worms. Instead, I accepted the redundancy package. I used the money to move to a place called Ozark, more rural and a suburb of Springfield. It was another normal, average, nice US town, surrounded by forests and mountains. It was classic middle-America which, as I learned over the years, was a good place to be anonymous. By that point I wasn't even in hiding. I looked over my shoulder occasionally and was always aware not to give anything away about my past but I certainly wasn't running.

In Ozark we had everything we needed and for a while we were comfortable. My payout from Nielsen provided us with money to live on and, although we weren't extravagant, we had a decent standard of living. With a few quid in the bank I reverted to my usual live-today philosophy and even started using a few credit cards, the bills for which soon added up. We hadn't bought property for years and continued to rent but when that started to reduce the savings I looked for another job and started to work for a company called Mediacom as a broadband technician. It was a step down because I was in upper management at Nielsen but it meant money and it was also a job that interested me. I had a cable van and started off in installation then moved up to a tech rep. I got on-the-job training and reached the heady heights of broadband technician level three – BBT3, to give it its industry acronym. Generally, I was happy doing the same as everyone else, working, putting money away, looking forward to retirement. But there never really seemed to be enough and so I relied more on credit cards and needed a few small loans. We downsized and moved to a smaller house and Debbie started working cash-in-hand for the leasing agent of our property, Brenda, who also became a valued friend. Debbie was in the office doing admin while I was out on the road, installing broadband.

One day I was on a job in someone's house when I heard a commotion outside. I looked out the window and saw a small crowd of people gathered around someone lying on the pavement. My first-aid instincts kicked in and I ran over to see what had happened.

'He's having a fit,' one of the bystanders explained.

The casualty was only a kid; a boy in his mid-teens. He was lying on the ground with his eyes rolling in their sockets and his body jerking. A bike was lying next to him. I assumed he'd fallen off.

'I'm a first-aider,' I said. 'Give me some room.' I knelt next to him and put him on his side, holding him firmly until the tremors stopped. I then checked his airway and put him in the recovery position. It looked to me as though he was suffering an epileptic fit. He had a head injury too. As I tried to talk to him to see if was responding I could feel him start to shudder again. I looked to my side and saw his leather wallet on the ground, which must have fallen out of his pocket. I grabbed it and put it in his mouth to stop him biting his tongue off.

'Has anyone called an ambulance?' I asked the crowd. Someone had and said it was on its way. I waited with the boy to make sure he was OK while the people around us looked on anxiously. The ambulance arrived after a couple of minutes. 'I think he's had an epileptic fit,' I explained. 'He's got an injury on the left side of his head too.'

I had a natural aversion to public scenes of drama so as soon as the paramedics strapped the kid on the gurney and wheeled him to the ambulance I slunk off quietly and went back to my work in the house over the road. I didn't think any more of it. I told Debbie, who teased me about being a local hero and then I forgot about it for a couple of days until I was called into the office by the area manager. He had someone with him who he introduced as the Mediacom PR officer.

'Were you working in Springfield the other day? Was it you who came across an accident?' she asked.

Warily, I nodded.

'That's great, Michael,' she gushed. 'The TV station wants to interview you. It will be great publicity for us.'

She explained that the kid's mum wanted to track down the good samaritan who had saved her son's life in order to thank him. In an effort to find me, the mother went to the local newspaper and the local TV station and asked them to put out an appeal, which I had missed. The woman whose house I had been working in at the time had called Mediacom to inform them that the life-saving cable guy the news channels were hunting for was one of their employees. They looked back at the log and saw that I was the technician on the job at the time. They were very excited about it all and had called the TV station to inform them. As all this was being explained to me, I was thinking, Oh, shit.

'Really, it was nothing. I'd rather not. Anyone would have done the same,' I explained.

'Michael, you are a hero. You saved that boy's life,' the PR women said.

'Honestly, it was nothing and I really don't want a fuss,' I persisted.

In the end, much to their disappointment, they had to go back to the TV channel and explain that the hero was indeed one of their own but that he was shy and didn't want to be identified because he wasn't an attention-seeker.

Another drama followed in 2008 when Debbie had a mild heart attack and needed to start taking medication. We were at home one evening and she started complaining of a tight chest. When she said she had pins and needles down her arm I called an ambulance and she was rushed in. Thankfully, it was a very minor attack and there was no damage but it shook us all up and we were warned that we had to be vigilant in the future.

Life carried on as normal but, with the reduced wages in my new position, I found it harder to make ends meet. I progressed through the levels but the work was still less well paid than at Nielsen. I moved to another company called SuddenLink to try and improve my earnings, doing the same work. Around the time I had several credit cards to service and, although I was managing to keep up repayments, I didn't want to start missing them and invite the scrutiny of the courts. I did some research and discovered that it would be easier to declare myself bankrupt than to be chased for money in the legal system. So that's what I did in May 2011.

I didn't know it at the time but these problems were omens of my eventual fate. 'Omen' is an apt word to describe the eventual architect of my downfall because, like in the movie, she was the bloody antichrist as far as I was concerned.

Lee had flitted back and forth in the intervening years and, in September 2011, he had one of the few bits of luck in his life when he won $100,000 on a scratchcard. At the time he was doing whatever he could for work. He had joined the volunteer fire brigade for a while and lived in one of their stations but that didn't last and he moved out. When he won the money – taxed at 25 per cent – he generally enjoyed himself, buying a truck (that he promptly crashed).

His sudden wealth didn't go unnoticed by the girlfriend of one of his friends, Jessica Butler. Lee fancied her and, like a fly to fruit, she fancied money. In my humble opinion she was one of those people who, if you threw some cash on the floor, would crawl on hands and knees to get it. Lee couldn't see it and I warned him but there's not a lot you can do when youthful hormones take over. She left her boyfriend and shacked up with Lee, creating bad feeling between him and his mate.

After just a few weeks, Lee ended up marrying her. It was a shock but given Lee's previous relationship history, it wasn't a surprise. She was a reasonable-looking girl but she was nothing special. Debbie and I went through the motions and went to the wedding. Jessica didn't work. She and Lee lived in Ozark not far from us. They never really settled and blew the money. We were always helping them out and once the money ran out they were always at our house, where we fed them. She became a millstone and their wedded bliss lasted all of a couple of months before they started rowing.

At that point, as far as I knew, Lee didn't know anything about my secret. He knew I couldn't go back to England and he knew I would be in trouble if I did but that was as much as I told him and, rather than accept the lack of knowledge, he filled in the blanks, using his own imagination. Apparently, he once told a girl I was a hitman. And then, from what I gather, when he was drunk one night he blurted out to Jessica that I was a fugitive. That must have set her off looking online and by then, of course, anyone could discover me with a few quick searches. I was using my own surname and there were photographs of me on old news reports. Jessica found me and finally the internet caught up with me. The thing I was putting in all over the state – the connection to the world wide web – was my undoing. I guess it was inevitable at some point because the internet made everyone more visible. Jessica read my name and she also saw the reward that had been offered. She sat on the knowledge for a while, during which time Lee and she continued to row. After one big argument she stormed off in a state and took a handgun with her that I'd bought Lee for his 22nd birthday. She complained about him to the police who went and arrested him and held him for traffic violations while she went to Ozark cop station where she grassed me up.

Records show that on 6 February 2012 – 19 years after I drove the Securicor van away – a woman walked into the police department and told an officer named David Overcast that she knew the whereabouts of the wanted British fugitive, 'Fast Eddie' Maher. She also made up a story that I had threatened to kill her and that she feared for her life. Officer Overcast didn't have a clue what she was talking about. No one in Missouri had ever heard of Fast Eddie. He punched my name into the police computer to see if I was wanted in any state in the US. I wasn't. Neither the name Eddie or Michael Maher registered as a person of interest. Even though the UK police had issued a statement on the fifth anniversary of the heist to say they suspected I was in the USA, the lead had never been followed up or, by the reaction of the police, made known to the US authorities. All that time on the run and no one was really looking for me.

So, instead of looking on the police database, officer Overcast went online instead and there he found me. I like to imagine that at the point when he realised he was sitting on the most sensational criminal case in Ozark police history, he dropped his donut in his coffee, but maybe I'm stereotyping. He immediately realised the seriousness and called the FBI who sensibly told him they would deal with things and make the arrest. In farcical fashion, he reportedly tried to call his counterparts in the UK, only to realise the police's phone contract did not allow officers to make international calls. Instead, he had to look online again, this time for the email address of Suffolk police.

Meanwhile, Lee was in the station and called me to tell me that he'd been nicked and that his loony lady had gone off with his gun. I got Debbie and Mark in the car and told them we were going to get Lee and warn the cops that there was a mad woman running around town with a shooter that perhaps she shouldn't have. I didn't want to go, but I was getting dragged into it. Lee was inside when I got there and I bailed him. Debbie and Mark stayed in the car. I bought Lee out and there were two policemen standing outside. I went over and started trying to explain to them about Jessica and the gun. I didn't want to sit down in the station and make a formal complaint for obvious reasons so I thought I'd have a quiet word with them, informally. They didn't seem to be interested and, as I was stressing my point, another copper pulled up in a car, heard what I was saying and asked me to follow him into the car park. I was agitated as it was but couldn't turn and run. He was in plain clothes, I didn't get his name but I started trying to explain to him about the stolen gun.

'Mr Maher, you've made your point,' he said. I wondered

how he knew my name. 'But what would you say if I told you that the lady you are complaining about has been to the police and reported that you are living here under a false name and you are wanted in England for a major crime and that the FBI are looking for you and that the only reason I'm not arresting you now is because they want to arrest you themselves in the next couple of days.'

BAM!

In that moment of further staggering police ineptitude, I knew the game was up, the cops told me so. Nineteen years of running and my past had finally found me. But I still couldn't quite work out if they were giving me a head-start to run again.

'I have no idea what you are talking about, officer,' I said, quick as a flash.

I don't know what he saw when he looked at me. I had got so used to lying I didn't think I showed any reaction. Inside, I was in turmoil. Oh, fuck, fuck, fuck, was all I was thinking. Outside, I shrugged and smiled and shook my head as if to say, 'You've got the wrong bloke, mate.' He just looked at me intently, waiting for me to crumble and offer him my hands to cuff. Instead I turned around and walked away.

I thought I was immune after all those years. My heart and mind were racing. I went back over to Lee. 'Come on, we're going,' I hissed. We got in the car and I didn't say a word. I was numb. It was obvious there was something wrong and Debbie asked what was happening.

'Nothing,' I said through a false smile. 'Let's go home.' We reached home and Lee and Mark got out of the car and went in. I touched Debbie's arm to slow her down on the pathway to the door. 'She's turned me in,' I said. 'The police know who I am. The feds are coming for me.'

Debbie started to mouth something but passed out. I caught her as she went down.

CHAPTER 17

BUSTED

The irony is that of all the places we lived in, Ozark was one of the best. It was affordable and, while it didn't have the affluence of New England, the pizzazz of Florida or the rugged beauty of Colorado, it was cosy and easy-going. It's where we would have retired, the final place on our flight from justice. While we were there I wasn't looking over my shoulder so much and I felt a little safer. I never allowed myself the luxury of thinking I had got away with it completely but I had certainly started to relax a little more.

All that went to shit. After I dragged Debbie in from the front path, sat her down and gently coaxed her back to consciousness, I made us a cup of coffee and tried to calm everything down. She was in tears and Mark and Lee were wondering what the hell was going on.

I sat the boys down and came clean. 'A long time ago in England I was forced into doing something that got me in a lot of trouble,' I explained. 'I was working for a company, delivering money and I drove away with the van. I had no choice at the time and there was quite a bit of money in it. To get you to safety, Lee, I sent your mum here with you and came over later. My identity was fake, it always has been. I'm wanted back in the UK for the crime and now the police and the FBI know who I am and where I am. I'm going to be arrested. I don't know what will happen after that but the chances are I'll get extradited to the UK.'

The boys looked at me with open mouths. Mark, bless his heart, had no idea at all. I felt like a complete bastard. His world was going to change completely. 'My real name is Eddie. Eddie Maher. And your mum isn't Sarah. She's Debbie,' I added. The news must have been shattering. 'Listen,' I went on. 'You all need to know that whatever happens, you will all be OK. None of you have done anything wrong. It is my mess. I am the one in trouble.'

It was important to reassure them that they would be safe.

'What's going to happen?' Mark asked. His voice was quivering.

I thought. Inside, I was thinking, Shit, what do I do now? I'd had the best part of two decades to come up with a plan B but I had no contingency. Mark was 14, Debbie had a heart condition, I wasn't a spring chicken any more. I couldn't be running around the country like an outlaw with a family; it was unfair and impractical. I guess I always knew that if it came to it, I'd go with my hands up and face the music. I had no money to get away anyway.

'I'll take what's coming to me and make sure you guys are OK,' I reassured. I needed time to think things through and to be with my family. Suddenly I was acutely aware that at any moment a team of cops could come crashing through the door and take me away from the people I loved and I had no idea for how long. For all those years, we'd been a solid unit – a team. They were my strength and I'd do anything for them. I wanted some breathing space and some time to think so I made a decision. 'Pack some stuff. We're going to a motel for the night,' I declared.

I didn't know it at the time but the house was under surveillance and there were FBI agents parked up in a car down the road. We left the house and got in our car. Lee went back to his home. Unknown to us, the feds followed us. Initially, they thought we were skipping town and going on the run but soon realised that we were only going a couple of miles up the road to the nearest motel. I booked us a room and we sat up for most of the night talking, answering Mark's questions and trying to comfort him. He was upset but he took it well and was amazing all the way through everything that followed. We told him everything. I told him about the theft and that no one was hurt. It was important for me that Mark didn't think I was some sort of violent thug. When he went to sleep Debbie and I discussed what we were going to do. Momentarily, we discussed running but I couldn't put them through the stress and I knew it was pointless. I was resigned to my fate.

That night I didn't sleep, neither did Debbie. After we'd said all there was we could say we lay together, exhausted and apprehensive, looking at the reflections of the car headlights on the ceilings as they passed outside, wondering if any of them were police cars coming to get us. In the morning, we were still free and so we checked out and drove around for a few hours, just to be together.

I called Lee and he told me that he'd been visited by the FBI and they had pulled him in for questioning. He told me that they knew everything and that they were going to arrest me imminently. He was upset. We went home briefly to pick up some more things and went back to the motel again. I wasn't running, I wanted to prolong the time I had left with Mark and Debbie and I wanted to get things straight in my head. I told Debbie that whatever happened I would do everything I could to make it easier for her. I tried to reassure her that she wouldn't get in trouble and that she'd done nothing wrong except overstay her visit. The worst they could do was deport her but Mark was a US citizen so that would be unlikely. I was aware of her medical condition and I didn't want her to have a heart attack.

The next morning, I knew it was pointless to keep moving around aimlessly. If the FBI were onto us we were most likely being watched and it was unfair on Mark. He needed normality and he needed to go back to school so we went back home, got his stuff together and took him. It was surreal. We were waiting for the inevitable and acting like a normal family on the school run. When I said goodbye to him I had a lump in my

BUSTED

throat because I realised that I might not be seeing him again for a long time. But I was relieved to get him to school; he was safe and away from what was about to happen.

We went back home and waited. We didn't have long. We made a coffee, had some food and I went upstairs to use the bathroom. As I sat in the toilet, merrily doing my business, there was a commotion outside and an aggressive banging on the door. 'Oh, well, at least I'm in the best place,' I said to myself with a sigh.

Debbie called up the stairs. 'They're here!' She sounded fraught. I heard the door open, a lot of loud voices and footsteps running up the stairs; lots of them.

In a second there was a rap at the toilet door.

'I'm in the toilet,' I called.

A gruff man answered. 'We have a warrant for your arrest. Come out.'

'Can you give me a second while I tidy myself up?' I asked.

'We're coming in,' he answered.

'Give me a second to finish off,' I pleaded.

I quickly did what I had to do, washed my hands and opened the door. There was a small platoon of law enforcement officers standing in a semicircle around the door. Some were carrying guns, others had rifles. I looked at them. They looked at me.

'I'd give that a minute if I were you,' I quipped.

In the bedroom, there were officers from the FBI and Immigration and Customs Enforcement (ICE). They were wearing flak jackets. I'm not sure what they were expecting and, although there were guns under the bed behind them,

213

Debbie and I were unlikely to do a Bonnie and Clyde. I got the impression they all wanted to be in on the bust. Outside there were about a dozen Ozark police officers and officers from the sheriff's department as well. In all there were around 30 or 40 cops from different agencies up the stairs, downstairs and surrounding the house. To be fair to most of them, they were good except for the FBI agents, who were arseholes.

I was led downstairs, where Debbie was in tears. I was asked for my wallet. The ICE agents wanted all my IDs. They took Debbie in the kitchen at the back of the house and asked her for her IDs too. While they were looking for documents that would prove who we were, the FBI cuffed me, put a chain around my waist and shackled my legs. They linked it all together and then led me clanking outside. They didn't read me my rights or tell me what they were arresting me for.

The leg irons and chains made it hard to lift my legs so I was helped over the doorstep. The front garden was full of uniforms. They were all standing around, looking a bit forlorn. Perhaps they were looking forward to a good, old-fashioned shoot-out or maybe they expected me to resist. They were probably a bit disappointed when they realised the UK's most-wanted criminal was a middle-aged, overweight, balding bloke.

Outside, one of the FBI blokes pulled me aside. 'Right, what's your real name?' he asked.

'Michael Maher,' I answered.

He leaned in and whispered in my ear. 'Look at your wife.' He nodded towards the window. I could see Debbie inside. She had calmed down a bit. 'She's safe and we are not going to arrest her. We'll keep her here and question her. We'll look after your boy at school too. All you need to do is tell me now who you are. If you don't we'll change all that. Make it easier for us and we'll make it easier for your family.'

'I'm Eddie Maher,' I admitted,

'You are Eddie Maher?'

'Yes,' I replied.

It was the first time in all those years I'd admitted who I was. I could have gone on for days telling them they had the wrong man but it wouldn't have done any good in the long run. They would have just put pressure on my family. I was the only one they were looking for and it wasn't fair to make it harder on Debbie and the boys.

The funny thing was that, even after all those years of running, it wasn't a weight off my mind to get caught. I had been living in fear precisely because I didn't know what was going to happen next. I knew I was going to get locked up and I'd seen stuff on TV about US jails. I didn't know what my legal position was, but I assumed I wouldn't get bail and I had no idea what kind of charges or sentence I was looking at.

After standing outside for about 20 minutes while the officers from ICE were getting all the documents together, the lead agent came over and spoke to me. She said, 'Your wife is OK. She's upset but OK. I know she's got a heart condition. We need to take her in to question her but we won't keep her in. She'll be on bail. We'll just book her and release her and we'll make sure Mark gets picked up from school. Everything will be fine.'

It was reassuring and a very decent thing to do. ICE were only concerned with immigration offences so they didn't treat me like a hardened criminal. They were actually human. The feds didn't have anything to charge me with so they handed me over to the ICE officers and the only charge they had on me was that I was an overstay; I was a suspected illegal immigrant. ICE put me in the back of their SUV. They took me to a town 15 miles away where they had an office and sat me down and processed me, which involved questions, forms, fingerprints, photos and DNA swabs. Debbie was taken there too and, although they kept us separate, the lead agent who had spoken to me at the house was brilliant and came over and explained that they were going to charge us both under the Immigration Act. They were going to keep me in but not Debbie, who was going to get bail and would have to report back.

'It doesn't matter what happens to me, as long as she and the boys are OK,' I said.

Before they let Debbie go they allowed me to say goodbye. They put us in a room together and we hugged. Debbie was in tears. I told her not to worry and that everything would be OK. It was hard. After all those years in which we'd led blameless lives it had all come crashing down. I didn't know it at the time, but that embrace was the last physical contact we would have for more than six months. The next time she saw me would be through a glass partition in a prison visiting centre where we could only speak to each other through a handset.

Debbie picked Mark up from school. It had only been a few

hours since the arrest but news had already got out and by the time she got him home there were journalists and TV crews outside the house.

Meanwhile, ICE wanted to know how I got into the country and what documents I used. The FBI bloke wasn't particularly interested in immigration matters so left the room. Lee had also been pulled in and they allowed him to come in and say goodbye too. He was upset. 'I don't know what to say, Dad.' It was hard for him. He'd split up with his wife, his family had all been arrested, he was an illegal immigrant. He was under a lot of stress. Lee never had a say in any of it.

During my time with ICE I had my first and only contact with the British embassy. I was handed a phone and there was a junior clerk on the other end. 'Is there anything we can do for you?' she asked.

'I need my British passport. Can you get it to me?' I asked. It would prove who I was and also help when I was inevitably extradited. 'I also need a lawyer and I want to make sure my wife and children are OK,' I added.

'We don't really deal with that,' the woman answered.

I was on my own. After processing and questioning I was taken to a holding cell, a big, long, open room with a bench down one side and a toilet in the corner. There was Spanish graffiti on the wall written in shit. I was on my own in there. There was a pile of blankets in case I fancied a kip, which I didn't. I sat for a while, contemplating everything, until one of the agents told me I was being taken to Christian County jail.

I had the uneasy feeling that I was in a process, being moved further into a system. Different agencies have contracts with different prisons. ICE had a contract with Christian County so immigration offenders went there. I later learned that the FBI had a contract with Green County jail. Inside Christian County I was put in a holding room awaiting processing. In each new facility it was the same. I went through the same tiring rigmarole: fingerprints, swabs, questions.

Here, the holding room was a long pen with two rows of metal benches on either side, one row above the other like in a sauna. There were 30 or 40 people in there. It was evening by then so it was mainly filled with those accused of drug offences with a few drunks thrown in for good measure. There were a few grubby mattresses. The door was metal and there was a small gap at the bottom that led into a gutter – that was the toilet. If you needed a piss you had to stand up and piss against the door. If you needed to do anything else you had to bang on the door and hope someone would come and take you to the facilities. The inmates were called out one at a time to be processed and then taken to cells on the main wings. It was like the worst doctor's waiting room in the world. There were already a couple of people in there who had seen me on the TV news. It was the first time I realised there had been reports about my arrest.

'You're famous,' one junkie slurred at me.

I waited in there and tried to avoid talking to anyone. Eventually, I was taken to the reception area where I went through the procedures and was then led into another holding cell that had bunks in it. With each step I was going further into the system and away from my nice cosy life.

I was taken into the shower. There was a hatch on the wall that was soon opened. The bloke behind it gave me a pile of prison clothes. 'Here's your underwear and your uniform,' he said. 'Strip off, place your clothes in the basket, bang on the wall when you want water.'

I was given shower shoes like Crocs – it was them or flip-flops and in the whole US jail system they are the only shoes prisoners can wear. I was given a plastic cup with a dollop of shampoo in it and a threadbare towel. I stripped, banged on the wall and showered briefly while I tried not to think about athlete's foot, verrucas and all the other infections that would have been crawling on the stone floor. The uniform was like hospital scrubs, its colour depending on the jail. In Christian County they were blue. In others they were green and federal prisoners got black-and-white stripes, which I was eventually given.

I showered and put on the clothes. I was fortunate enough to get a new pair of pants – well, that's what I told myself. They put me in a four-man holding cell which was full. I weighed up who was who. Most of them were junkies. That was true in most of the places I ended up in; prisons are full of junkies and people with a lot of psychological problems. I climbed on the nearest available bunk – a solid sheet of steel, like a shelf. I had been given a thin mattress, a sheet and a blanket. There are no pillows in US jails. I had the roughest night of my life.

The next day the FBI finally charged me, although all they could get me on was illegal possession of firearms. While I'd bought the guns over the counter with my ID, all my documents were fake. The agents shackled me again and took me to Springfield courthouse. By then the media circus was in overdrive and reporters congregated on the courtroom steps, wanting to get the first picture of me in almost 20 years. In recognition of my admitting my real identity the agents didn't make me do the walk of shame and instead took me in through the back of the building where I was put in another cell. After a while I was manacled and taken into a small court room. There were just a few people with a judge and clerk at the front. The charges were read out and I was refused bail. I didn't have to say anything or plead. It was just a formality – a part of the process.

As I was then a federal prisoner who belonged to the FBI, I was taken to another jail, Green County, which was in Springfield and much bigger than Christian County. It held hundreds of prisoners. It wasn't as big as the state and federal penitentiaries but some cons were serving out their full terms. I went through the same process in Green County. The showers were even worse. I got a uniform again, this time the black-and-white stripes. As if the news reports were not bad enough, I now looked like a zebra and wandered into my new environment like easy prey.

CHAPTER 18

NOT-SO-FAST EDDIE

While I was getting acquainted with my new surroundings, Debbie and Mark were having their own battles with the media. Mark's school had been informed by the police about events and, on the day of the arrest, they put measures in place to protect him and to keep any reporters who turned up at bay.

In the US, schools have security guards and the one at Mark's took charge of the situation and beefed up patrols around the school grounds. When Debbie went to pick up Mark, the guard explained that if reporters did start to make things difficult, he would take Mark out of class, dress him up in the school mascot costume, put him in the back of the squad car that he drove and drive him home. The guard was armed with a gun and a taser and was authorised to use force to protect pupils. He took his duties seriously and Debbie was reassured to know that Mark would have an armed guard if needed.

She got Mark home, where she had to negotiate a throng of reporters who had staked us out. They stayed for days hoping for a quote, interview or a photo and Mark and Debbie couldn't get out of the front door for a week so Mark had to have time off school. Each time they went to leave they were met with a barrage of clicking cameras and questions. The people on the estate where we lived were brilliant and fended them off as best they could. Eventually, the press pack realised they weren't getting anything and one by one their editors called them off.

The news cycle moved on and when Debbie thought the coast was clear she tried to get Mark back to school. She got him in the car but a few yards down the road another car pulled behind them and a photographer in the passenger seat started taking pictures. They followed Debbie to the school and into the car park. She pulled up by the door, grabbed Mark, ran in and went straight to the guard who ran out to warn them off. As soon as they saw him they drove away. When Debbie left after dropping Mark off she was followed by the same car but managed to manoeuvre through several side streets and lost the pursuing vehicle. She later discovered it was a French journalist and photographer. In the subsequent report, they wrote that Debbie would have made a good getaway driver.

Meanwhile, I stayed in Green County jail for four months. I had no idea when I first got there how long I'd be in for or what was going on. I soon got the impression that the authorities were equally confused. The US federal government were holding me on trumped-up firearms charges as a favour for the Home Office in the UK which wanted to prosecute me for the Felixstowe job. I imagined that the UK would be doing all it could to get me back to Blighty ASAP. But it wasn't. In order to leave the US, I needed a valid passport. As a UK citizen, I had the right to a passport, but the Passport Office adopted the attitude of a spoilt brat and did all it could to hold up the process. One official even told me, 'Why should we help you? It was your choice to run away.' So I languished in jail while the Passport Office metaphorically sat at the back of the classroom with its arms crossed in defiance.

It wasn't an enjoyable wait. Jails aren't designed to be pleasant places and Green County was no exception. It was laid out like a rimless wheel: there was a central hub control room with the wings designed as the spokes radiating from it. This made it easier for the guards to control the population. They could look down the corridors and see what each wing was up to. Each of the four wings – called 'green', 'red', 'blue' and 'white' – had several floors and prisoners were assigned to them depending on their status and crime. Prisoners wore non-removable wristbands on which was recorded name, number and wing. I was on green (for vulnerable prisoners; red wing was for violent offenders).

The first thing that surprised me was that prison officers did not mix or interact with prisoners. Everything was controlled electronically via CCTV and loudspeaker. The guards were in the hub, behind glass. All the doors were operated remotely.

Coloured lines painted on the floor were used to move prisoners through the prison. I'd be told what to do by an announcement made over the loudspeaker in the cell. 'Maher, go to the blue line.'

I'd walk to the blue line by the cell door. The guard in the hub was watching me all the time over the camera in the cell and he would then buzz the door open. I'd step through and then be given my next instruction. 'Maher, go to the blue line at the end of the corridor.'

It was a strangely dehumanising process that was designed to reinforce the feeling of alienation and isolation from the outside world. Why didn't my cellmate run away when the door was opened? Because there was nowhere to go. Anyone trying to escape could only ever get as far as the next locked door. The whole system negated the need for guards to walk around with keys and made sure the prisoners were securely caged where the guards wanted them.

Cells were supposed to house two men but they were always overcrowded. When a third prisoner arrived he was given what they called a boat, a plastic, flat-bottomed coffin-like bed with a mattress in it. The boat went on the floor. Inside the cells there was a toilet and a wash basin in the wall and a speaker. There were shelves but no lockers because prisoners had no possessions apart from the books they could borrow from the library cart. The toilet, which was stainless steel, was open. If you used it, everyone could see, which was just about acceptable for pissing but was unpleasant for anything else, particularly if you needed to go in the middle of the night.

Most cells rigged up temporary curtains using blankets but the control room always demanded they got taken down for surveillance purposes; every part of every cell needed to be visible at all times. In my cell we tried to preserve some decorum and waited until the others were out. Elsewhere some people didn't care and would go as and when they wanted. It was a point of friction for many inmates.

In the early hours of one morning, after I'd been there for about a week, I was in bed when the speaker crackled to life. 'Maher, go to the blue line,' ordered an emotionless voice. I got out of my bunk, bleary-eyed and stepped up to the line. The door buzzed open. I stepped out and was told by the loudspeaker to go to the next line. The process took me through the prison to the medical wing. At one point I was told to go to an elevator. There was no button to call it. The door opened and I stepped inside. It closed behind me. I waited for several minutes in silence before the door behind opened again.

'Maher, step out the elevator,' the voice said.

I did.

'Maher, go to the red line on your left.'

I did as I was told and a door in front of me opened.

'Maher, climb up the stairs three flights.'

I realised the lift wasn't working. Eventually, I was led into the medical centre and was told to wait in a room where – at last – a human being appeared. He handcuffed me and led me through to a room with doctors and nurses waiting. It looked like a normal hospital and was quite a surreal sight, given where I had just come from. I asked what was happening and was told I was there for a medical.

'It's 3am!' I exclaimed.

'This is a 24-hour operation. We have to fit a lot of people in.' They checked me over and told me I had high blood pressure.

'No shit, Sherlock! You get me up at 3 am and make me climb three flights of stairs, what do you expect?' I explained. So they waited, checked again and confirmed that it was still high so they put me on blood pressure medication, which was the one good thing that came out of my time there.

My cell was on the ground floor and there were three tiers on my wing. In front of the cells there was a communal area with tables and plastic stacking chairs lined up along the walls. They were designed to be hard and uncomfortable. We were locked in at night but we were fairly free to come and go within the space as often as we wanted. On the wall at the end of the communal area, ten feet up, there was a 22-inch television. The choice of channels was designated by the sheriff. There were never any shows with violent or sexual content so as not to excite the inmates. There were no police shows and no Jerry Springer. Instead we had folk music channels, some soaps and documentaries. Some inmates stood around all day watching the box. I thought, Why bother? Fortunately, I read a lot so I read books and I also talked, went to meals and cleaned the cell. The exercise area was also on the wing, indoors; it was just a big, empty room that you walked around. There was no canteen. I never went out of the wing. The inmates who worked in the kitchen came to the end of the wing with trays of food at meal times, each tray like a budget airline meal. I would also get a spork and could either go to a table or get another chair and use that to eat off.

The food was carefully measured to provide just enough calories and nutrition to survive and everyone got the same meal. Even the fries were measured to make sure everyone had an equal portion. People got obsessed with food and an unequal share of fries could easily spark a prison riot. My favourite meal was corn dogs – hot-dog sausages covered in batter. Each inmate got two. In the outside world a corn dog came on a wooden stick but in jail someone could make a shank from it – or maybe collect a load and fashion some kind of escape vehicle, like in *The A-Team*. Milk for cereal and orange juice came in little cartons and I tried to keep one of them back each day for later, just to have something to look forward to. Saving food was against the rules however, so it was a gamble. We were supposed to hand back anything we didn't finish.

The prison opened a commissary account for me on my arrival. Debbie could put money in it each week and I could buy extra goods from a designated list. Mainly, commissary meant food and it was a vital lifeline for most inmates because, no matter who you were, you lost weight. I was hungry most of the time, but people with no money in commissary got in a really bad way. The purchases were delivered at the end of each week in a bag and there was no limit to how much we could buy, although it was better to set a limit as fellow inmates would steal. I bought sweets and chocolate but never flaunted what I had.

In the US there is a company that caters solely for commissary in prisons. Some of what they provided was really good, like the big bags of spicy chips that were cheap. There were also packs of army-style rations, such as processed boil-in-the-bag soy and refried bean chilli. In my cell we clubbed together. One of us got the chilli, another got tortilla wraps and someone else the chips. We saved whatever meat we got from our meal in the day and at night we 'cooked' and made tortilla wraps. Prisoners didn't get hot drinks but we could buy tea and coffee through commissary and request a jug of hot water. We used the jug to warm the ration packs and wrapped them up in blankets to keep them hot.

Soon after I went in to Green County I met my public defender (PD), the lawyer tasked with representing me. He had an investigator called Mark who worked with him and was my main contact. In our first meeting, they confirmed that I was being held because the UK had asked for me to be extradited and the FBI had only come up with firearms charges. On the other side of the legal fence was the district attorney, the prosecutor. He was an elected official and I think he wanted to make a name for himself because he went to the grand jury while I was being held and added another couple of charges – possession of false ID and using a false ID to gain employment. The possession charge was nothing, but the employment charge carried a mandatory two-year sentence. The UK authorities were perfectly happy to let me have jail time in the US and then when I'd done that and was deported they would jail me again in the UK. It didn't look good.

As the weeks went by I made a few friends and learned more about my fellow inmates and what some of them were in for. There was an etiquette inside: you didn't ask so much as wait until others offered you information. We did have a lot of time in there and it would inevitably turn up in conversation. Inmates also gossip and after a week or so most people on the wing knew who I was. Mainly they were friendly. Often people would come up to me and exclaim excitedly: 'You are a legend! You are all over the TV.' Prisoners wanted to be associated with me. I became notorious quite quickly and had only been inside a day or so when I got asked the question that I would be asked hundreds of times since. 'Where's the money?'

One of the guys I was in with had been in jail quite a few times. His name was Dave and he was a drug-pusher but a nice enough bloke. He took me under his wing and showed me the ropes. One day I was eating with my tray on a chair in front of me when some young kid with a real temper stormed past and kicked the chair, spilling the slop I was eating. He was angry about something and was shouting and swearing. Dave pulled him aside, put his arm around him and had a chat. The youngster then came over to me and said he was sorry and that he didn't mean any offence. 'I'm just having a really hard time,' he explained.

'That's all right, mate, we all have bad days,' I said. Later I asked Dave what he'd said to the kid.

'I just told him he needed to calm down and that we are not in a school yard. This is not the place to do shit like that, otherwise you might end up getting hurt. There are different levels of people in here. And I told him you are a legend,' he laughed.

Inmates tended to congregate in racial groups. The blacks and the whites stayed to themselves and rarely mixed. There were a couple of skinheads next to me in a cell and they were really nice. They were both covered in tattoos with a prominent design around the letters 'AN' on their necks, marking them out as members of the white supremacy organisation Aryan Nations. They told me to make sure I let them know if I was having any problems and I thought they were trying to recruit me. I thanked them politely but didn't take them up on their offer.

There were regular fights and, whenever it kicked off, the guards went in quick and hard. If it was bad enough they maced the culprits. I always knew when there was violence, even on another wing, because the mace fumes stung my eyes and made me cough. The guards dragged out those involved in whatever way they could. They didn't pussyfoot around and weren't worried about hurting people. It was an unsettling sight. Prisoners fighting who didn't calm down were dragged to isolation where they were stripped naked and put in surgical smocks. They were laid out on a big wooden bed, face down, then handcuffed and shackled so they couldn't move, no matter how much they thrashed around. Depending on how violent they were, a nurse from the medical wing administered syringes of the drug Thorazine in their arse; bang, bang, bang – one after the other. The inmate was then left, zonked out until they calmed down. If they woke up and were still going they would be thorazined again. The ones who were slightly calmer were put in a rubber cell for a few days to think about what they had done. It was the hard-core equivalent of a naughty step.

Even with drama like that, prison was boring. It wasn't supposed to be entertaining. It was designed to place inmates in a mundane routine where every day was the same. The only link to the outside world was a single, blue plastic phone on the wall of the wing that we could use at certain times and that I'm sure was monitored. The air con was on as cold as it could get and pointed straight at the phone. My teeth chattered by the time I had reached the end of the queue and I didn't stay on it for long. It was just another little form of torture to make our life as uncomfortable as possible.

People moan that prisoners have it easy, that they sit around all day, watch TV and get fed. They forget that people don't get sent to prison to be punished. Prison is the punishment. It keeps you away from your family and your life. Being in prison isn't an excuse to then further torture someone. The punishment is deprivation of liberty. You are nothing. You are part of a process. Your free will is taken away. That's the punishment.

I settled in to prison life and tried to keep my head down and remained stoic about my situation. I spoke to Debbie often on the phone and she assured me her and Mark were OK. In an effort to try and keep my spirits up, she didn't tell me about the troubles she was having and I didn't tell her how shit prison was, for the same reason.

After a couple of weeks another bloke came into our cell. I had the top bunk at the time. The bottom was better because you could close it off and you didn't have to climb up. Dave had that because he was in first. The new bloke, Jim, got a boat, which was bad. He was a bit older than me and it was his first time inside. He cried a lot. The courts had hammered him with an incredibly long sentence. He was a farmer and when they raided his property they found a load of cannabis plants and several thousand dollars in his safe. He was in shock – he wasn't a hardened criminal, he was a family man who had diversified his crop. He got 35 years and knew he might never go home again.

Dave tried to calm him down. 'Don't worry, you'll be all right. You won't do all that time. You have to man up, don't dwell on it all the time,' he advised. But the bloke was in a bad way. In a quiet moment, Dave pulled me aside and said, 'He won't last. He'll kill himself.' In prison, defiance and denial don't get you far. Ask any inmate and they'll tell you they are the innocent victim of some terrible miscarriage of justice. Most of them don't believe it, though. The ones that do will slowly go mad. To survive, you need a bit of Zen – you need to let prison wash over you and allow yourself to move along in the system. You lose a bit of your soul in the process but you keep your sanity. Eventually, Jim calmed down and started to accept his faith. I learned to take the little victories where I found them. Dave helped me see prison from that perspective. A corn-dog day was a good day. A cooking evening was a good evening. A call to Debbie was a blessing.

After about a month, Dave got out. He had been on parole when he was arrested and thought that was it, that he would never get out again but they granted him new parole and released him. I was sorry to see him go, but using his philosophy looked at it as a positive and moved down to the bottom bunk. Jim moved up to the top and all was well in the cell. I was lying there that night, feeling quite content when the loudspeaker barked to life.

'Maher, come to the blue line, bring your possessions and your bedding.'

I frowned. If I needed my possessions, it meant I was going. I gathered up my clothes and my toothbrush (standard issue with a short rubber handle to ensure it couldn't be turned into a shiv). I rolled up my sheets and mattress and I stood by the line, looking at Jim who looked at me and then looked at the top bunk, before smiling for the first time. His day had just gone from good to better.

I was led out of the wing through a door where two sheriffs were waiting. For a split second I thought I was getting out. One of the sheriffs asked for my arm so I put the stuff down and held out my hand, expecting cuffs. Instead, he cut off the plastic bracelet and replaced it with a black one. I was being moved to the solitary wing. I was shocked. It was a punishment.

'What the hell! What have I done?' I was incredulous.

'Don't know, we are just here to move you,' one answered. They led me to the solitary confinement wing, a corridor lined with single cells. The area outside had no chairs because there was no association – there was only the big wooden bed in the middle where the violent prisoners were strapped. At the end there was an exercise area, about 12 foot by 12 foot. There was nothing in it. Opposite there was another row of cells, the rubber rooms. The tier above housed the inmates who worked in the prison; they were called trustees and worked the kitchens and the laundry room. On the other side of their cells at the top of the wing was the PC (protective custody) corridor.

I was placed in a cell furnished with a single bed, a hand-basin and a toilet. I had no idea what was going on – you only got solitary if you did something wrong. I spent a sleepless night worrying about the situation and the next morning was picked out and taken to see the warden. My public defender and his assistant were there too. The warden was a real stereotype. He sat behind a big wooden desk chewing the end of a big cigar. Mark asked if I was OK. I explained what had happened and the warden cleared his throat.

'We had to move you because you have become notorious and there has been a lot of interest. We moved you into solitary for your own safety.' He threw a big wad of envelopes on the desk in front of me. I leafed through them; *Good Morning America*, the *New York Times*, the *National Inquirer*. They were letters asking for an interview. 'A couple have put money into your commissary account. We can't have it. We can't have you in general population.'

I protested that I'd done nothing wrong and that it was unfair. I knew there were rules in solitary that the officers controlling the wing stuck to. Inmates could not get out to use the phone and had no association time. I wasn't too bothered about association but I explained that I would not be able to call home and let people know what was going on and also reiterated that I was on remand and hadn't been sentenced. In the eyes of the law I was innocent until proven guilty.

The PD pleaded my case and the warden listened. 'OK,' he said finally. 'I'll tell you what I'll do. I'll allow you out of the cell each night at eight to make your calls and your visiting rights will be unchanged.' Debbie had been visiting once a week. Each visit lasted 15 minutes and we spoke on either side of a window on a telephone.

I continued to protest over the following days and there were further discussions. The warden came up with another plan. 'The only other option is to put you on the protective custody wing,' he said. I didn't know what that was. 'It's where prisoners who have turned state evidence and the like are housed. The system is the same as general population but they are kept in their own unit.' Without realising then what 'and the like' meant, I agreed.

I was sent back to my solitary cell while the arrangements were made and later that day a guard came to me with a form to sign. It was like a contract. One of the clauses stated, 'I understand that if I lay hands on anyone while I am in protective custody I will receive an automatic five-year prison sentence'.

I thought it was severe but realised that grasses were targets and as I signed my name I absent-mindedly muttered: 'Is this to protect the mafia super-grasses then?'

The guard laughed.

'No! It's to protect the chomos.'

'The what?' I frowned.

'Chomos – child molesters. You're going on their wing,' he said.

And with that, I was taken, protesting furiously and put in with the nonces, the last place I wanted to be. Fortunately, there were also a couple of grasses in there who were avoiding the mob and so I hung out with them, which wasn't ideal but at least they weren't perverts. I repeatedly asked to go back into general population but my requests were refused. The reason given was my notoriety. In another demonstration of administrative pointlessness, every week I was given a 'contract' in which I was supposed to specify whether I wanted to remain in protective custody or return to general population. Mine was already filled in for me and I had no choice in the matter but was told to sign the paperwork anyway. Mainly, I kept myself to myself and only had to mix with the others when I went down to get my meal tray.

I had a single cell and spent most of the time in it reading. The trustees knew who I was and why I was there so, thankfully, I didn't get bodily fluids deposited in my meals like the chomos. Trustees even asked the guards if I could be transferred into their wing. There was a door between the two wings and the trustees started passing newspaper cuttings of me to autograph. I signed them 'Not So Fast Eddie' and they passed them outside during visits to friends and family who sold them on Ebay.

Showers on the wing were open, so the guards could watch

and make sure no one was up to anything or being shanked. As a result, everyone on the balcony opposite and above could see down into the shower unit. I did a double-take myself when, looking down, I saw someone in profile with long hair and a curvy figure. They also had a pair of tits. I stopped in my tracks. It was the last thing I expected to see inside a prison and wondered if it was some kind of mirage. I stood there, blinking at the vision below for a few seconds until the person turned around fully and stepped out of the cubicle revealing that, below the waist, he was all man!

I had regular meetings with the PD; it became apparent that the US authorities were not interested in prosecuting me. I was in limbo, simply waiting for the UK justice department to arrange my extradition. I asked if the time I was spending on remand in the US would come off the eventual sentence, as would normally be the case. The PD said he doubted it because I would be back in the UK. 'So, if they are holding me on a charge here while they wait to extradite me and it's not coming off a sentence in the UK, in effect I'm doing extra jail time for nothing,' I said. He nodded. 'Well, send me to the airport and I'll pay my own fare home. I'm not going to wait for extradition if it is not coming off a sentence at the other end. Let me go back home and face the music.'

The PD said he'd take the suggestion to the DA. They hummed and hawed about it for weeks until the DA announced that he had an idea. 'We will take Mr Maher to the airport and allow him to go back under his own volition and face the charges in the UK,' he said, taking credit for my suggestion. As I was returning home voluntarily the justice department said that as soon as I was on the plane the charges against me in the US would be dismissed. I never went to court in the USA and I was never convicted of any offences there.

The FBI now knew they were not going to secure a conviction and didn't need to pay for me to be held in Green County. They handed me over to ICE who only had the immigration charges. First the feds took me to court to formally drop their charges. I was taken back to Springfield courtroom where the formalities were performed in front of a judge.

'Mr Maher, you are released on bail,' he said.

I sat in the courtroom, still shackled, waiting for ICE to come and pick me up. I turned to the PD. 'I can go now? I'm on bail.'

He laughed. 'Technically... yes,' he said.

'Do you think I'll be able to get out the door quicker than they can catch me in these leg irons?' I spent about an hour as a 'free man' before agents from ICE came and took me back to Christian County jail. It had been almost four months since my arrest. All that time my family had to survive without me. Debbie was in dire straits. She had no passport or ID and was given a date when she was told she either had to be out of the country or appear before an immigration judge who would decide whether she would be deported or allowed to stay. She was also told she wasn't allowed out of the state of Missouri to apply for a passport through the UK embassy. She suffered more than I did. At least I knew my fate, even if that was going to prison in the UK. She didn't know what was going to happen to her or to Mark. And to make matters worse, Mark was having problems getting a passport.

My family in the UK had seen the reports in the papers and they started to get in touch. For most of us it was a bittersweet reunion. A few of them were glad to hear from me and a few of them haven't spoken to me to this day. I saw Terry again after more than 20 years. He was one of the ones who really helped us out. He even came over to the USA to help, which was appreciated. He was now a man in his 30s but I recognised him straight away. I apologised and tried to explain the whole saga. He told me no apology was needed. There were plenty of downsides to being captured but the reunion with family was one of the positive things. After six months in jail in the USA I was finally homeward bound, returning to London town.

CHAPTER 19

HOMEWARD BOUND

By July 2012, apart from the move from Christian County to Green County and back again via court, I had not been outdoors and sniffed fresh air or seen natural daylight for six months. It took a while for my senses to get used to it when I was led outside and put in a car to go to the airport.

When the time for my extradition had come, it happened suddenly. I got an indication the night before that something was afoot because I wasn't allowed to use the phone and the guards went all mysterious on me when I asked, which set alarm bells ringing. Prisoners never got told when they were being moved. It was one of the little psychological tricks used to keep us on our toes. I went to sleep that night hoping that Debbie would call in the morning to get some information. She knew how the process worked too and had been warned that the authorities were likely to move me at a moment's notice without informing her. She'd taken to calling the prison switchboard each morning and sometimes in the afternoon to ask after me. The receptionist knew her well and they were friendly as a result.

In the morning I was taken off the wing into a room where I was met by three US marshals, who explained they were there to escort me back to the UK. It wasn't a surprise. I was half-glad that finally something was happening and half-apprehensive because I didn't know whether Debbie was aware of the situation – which she wasn't. It was like rendition. I was getting spirited out of the country and no one knew. I was given the bag of clothes that Debbie had left for me weeks previously when I first arrived. They were my old clothes and after six months on prison rations they didn't fit. I had lost around 50 pounds. Thankfully, I had a belt.

I was allowed a shower, got changed and was shown a piece of paper that explained I was being deported and handed over to the authorities in England. One of the marshals leaned into me and, with coffee-breath, asked, 'Are you going to be a problem? If you are we'll cuff you. If not, you can travel normally.' I told him I'd be quiet as a mouse and they put me in the car and took me to Springfield Airport. I was handed over to two new marshals and given another sheet of paper to show I was being removed from the country of my own volition as a result of immigration issues. I would not be able to re-enter the USA for five years. The justice system loves a document. Every move through it, each fart, everything requires a piece of paper that needs to be signed.

Springfield was a quiet airport and we were booked on a domestic flight to Chicago where we'd catch a connection to Heathrow. They didn't tell me the route at the time, though. I felt like a school kid as I queued up between my escorts to get a boarding pass. When we stepped up to the desk they spoke for me and handed over my tickets. We boarded and were assigned seats right at the back. I sat between the two men and watched Springfield and the mountains beyond slip away, wondering what Debbie and Mark were doing. I felt sick in my stomach. They were to be left in the US and I didn't know whether they would ever get to the UK. Nor did they. It was playing on my mind all the time. I was totally useless to them and it was frustrating. I was a family man and had provided for my family all my life. Suddenly I was deprived of the ability to do that. The helplessness was the main punishment. I couldn't support them and was particularly worried because I knew Debbie wasn't well. Thankfully she had people who were helping her.

At O'Hare International airport I waited in the lounge with the rest of the travellers. One of the marshals explained that they had a budget for food and that they were obliged to get lunch for me.

I looked around and saw the golden arches. 'Can I get a McDonald's?'

'Sure,' he said. The three of us sat together and ate burger and fries. It was the first non-prison meal I'd had since my arrest and it was undeniably good. I tried to make conversation to pass the time as they were quite nice blokes. Technically, I wasn't a prisoner but they told me that I still wasn't allowed a beer, which was a shame.

On the flight we were given the rear seats again and I watched a few movies and tried to relax. It was obvious to the rest of the passengers what was going on because I was accompanied to the toilet each time. But the flight was uneventful and when we landed we waited until everybody else got off, when a couple of blokes came to the back of the plane and introduced themselves as Met Police officers. 'Please come with us Mr Maher,' they said.

We all walked off together and at the end of the gangway, in the terminal, the marshals handed over their paperwork and a clear plastic folder. Inside I could see all my IDs. I was handed over to the UK police and the marshals said their goodbyes and walked off for what I assumed would be a couple of days in London. The two plain-clothes coppers read me my rights and led me in the opposite direction, through the airport to a waiting car that took me to a police station where I was formally charged with the 1993 theft.

Meanwhile, back in Ozark Debbie at least knew what had happened. She got up as normal and made her call and was told I was still there but, at 1pm, as I was boarding the flight to Heathrow, she got a call from the investigator who told her to call the jail. He'd got wind that something had happen. She called and got a hard time because it wasn't the usual woman on the switchboard. Eventually, they admitted to her that I'd gone. She called Terry in the UK and he lined up legal help for my arrival.

Over the following weeks, Debbie was kept informed of my movements and we spoke on the phone. She continued to battle the bureaucracy to get out of the US with Mark. She was herself under threat of deportation and had also been charged with immigration offences. She was given until 30 August to get out of the US under her own free will. If she didn't, she would be arrested and could be jailed for up to two years. Yet the UK government continued to stall on giving her a passport. Finally, after a lot of begging, she was issued with one on 9 August. She also struggled to get a passport for Mark because the authorities in America questioned his parentage as we'd used assumed identities when we registered his birth. I got the impression the authorities, particularly in the UK, were making it unnecessarily hard for them and that angered me. You don't punish the sons for the sins of the fathers.

It was weird for me to be hearing English accents everywhere. It was all very formal: the coppers in Heathrow hardly spoke to me. In the police detention centre I was fingerprinted, photographed and a DNA swab was taken from inside my cheek. In the US they asked to take a DNA sample but in the UK there were no such niceties. I didn't have the right to refuse. People in the UK don't even realise how few rights they actually have.

After being formally charged I was told I was being taken to HMP Norwich, the nearest prison to the crime scene. The case would be heard in Norwich Crown Court. First, I was taken to a court to begin the process. There were four coppers in the front of the van and a cage in the back for me.

I was on my own and handcuffed. We drove around the back of the court and I was taken down to the cells to wait to be called in by the judge. I was still in same clothes I changed into the morning I left Christian County. I was slightly jet-lagged and disorientated. A court guard came and got me and led me up into the court room where the beak formally remanded me in custody.

My legal representative accompanied me. I had been given legal aid and my family had arranged for me to be represented by a firm in London but, because the hearing was a formality, the London firm had employed a local solicitor. He did his best to request bail for me and explained that members of my family were willing to put up their houses as surety, but the judge rejected the request. Technically, I should have got it because I had returned to the UK voluntarily so was not a flight risk. I soon got used to the fact that the Ministry of Justice was not too bothered about bending the rules when it came to my case. I also think the judge believed the hype and assumed that, because I'd managed to evade capture for 20 years, I was a Houdini-like figure who would disappear without a trace again given half the chance. No one wanted to accept the truth, which was that the police hadn't tried very hard to find me and the reason I got away with it for so long was because they were crap at their jobs.

From Norwich Crown Court I was put in one of the cubicles in a Serco van and driven to my new home. Everything felt alien. Outside, I got glimpses of the country through the van window and I didn't recognise anything. All the cars were small and there were a lot more takeaways than I remembered. I wasn't English, I was American; I felt like a foreigner.

HMP Norwich was an imposing Victorian building. The reception centre was in a separate building where I was searched and put on an X-ray chair that took an image up my arsehole so the guards could see whether I was smuggling anything. It's a bit like an electric chair. All prisons have them. After that I was sent to an open cell to wait before being called up to give my details and check my charges. The commissary in the UK is called the canteen and I was asked if I wanted anything. New prisoners were given a little starter pack with a few goods and snacks in to tide them over before they set up an account. I was asked if I was a smoker. If I had been, the state would have provided me with a small pouch of tobacco because in UK jails, prisoners were allowed to smoke. It was unlike the US, where county jails were smoke-free. I took my pack and was offered my first meal on UK soil, microwaved sausage, mash and gravy, eaten with a plastic knife and fork, standing up. It was quite nice.

I was taken to the reception wing that was mainly for remand prisoners. I was allowed to keep my bag of clothes and was given a blanket. The wing was the newest in the prison and was supposed to be a temporary place where new inmates adjusted to prison life or waited for sentencing after trial, but because the prison system was so overcrowded, some inmates with short sentences stayed there. British prison guards – or screws, as they were affectionately called – mixed with prisoners in the wing. The difference was that cons were mainly free to walk around the wings in the US and we spent more time locked up in the UK.

Along with another bloke who had been processed with me, I was taken through a series of cages to get into the corridor with my cell. The layout was much the same as in the US, each wing spread out over a number of mezzanine floors that all opened around a central space. There were safety nets between each floor to lessen the risks if inmates threw objects or themselves over the balconies. The corridors were lined with cells. Each floor held a specific type of prisoner.

I was taken to a cell and the guard unlocked the door and opened it. As he did, a cloud of cigarette smoke wafted out. It was horrible. 'Don't even think about it,' I said, shaking my head. 'Please don't put me in with a smoker, it's disgusting.' Fortunately, they put the other guy in there and put me in a non-smoking cell further down the corridor. There were no guarantees that a smoker wouldn't go in with a non-smoker but they did try and match people up to avoid conflict and possibly any lawsuits launched by a cancer-suffering non-smoking ex-con. There was another man in the cell I was shown into who had already bagged the bottom bunk, which was fair because he was in first.

My bunk was slightly more comfortable than those I had been used to in the USA. The mattress was about an inch thicker and was covered in blue plastic to make it pee-proof. I also got a little pillow and a quilt. I looked at my new surroundings. The toilet in the corner had a little curtain that didn't reach the floor. There was a pin-board on the wall and a TV in the room with a lot of Freeview channels, including movie channels, which was a real bonus. Mainly prisoners loved soaps and soccer (or football, as I had to call it again).

I introduced myself to my cellmate, John. Absent-mindedly I looked out the door at the floor above and saw a line of inmates shuffling in a queue to a dispensary trolley. Each one was given a tiny paper cup full with what looked like Fairy Liquid. 'What's going on there?' I asked John.

'Methadone time,' he said. 'They get it the same time each day. They get more if they make a fuss.'

I was shocked. The junkies were all on their own corridor and were medicated every day. It was the first time I'd seen the extent that drugs had a hold on the prison population in the UK. Each one of the addicts drank their dose and shuffled back to their cell. If you were a junkie in the States, you either go cold turkey or are taken out of general population and treated.

Over the following days I discovered that people got locked up on purpose to get their drugs. It happened every November. They came in because it was warmer and because they liked spending Christmas inside. There are hundreds of people who purposefully commit crimes in October and November and deliberately get caught knowing the sentence they will get. They get Christmas dinner, drugs and are released for the January sales. Every prison in the UK starts filling up in the festive run-up. For many people, prison is not a punishment; there are those who use the system to their benefit.

John showed me the ropes around Norwich nick and he became a good friend over the following days. Every prisoner was expected to do a job and if we worked we got money in our canteens. If we didn't, we got 50p a week unemployment benefit. John got a job in the servery after a week or so which then entitled him to have a single cell across the wing. Job allocation was decided by the wing No. 1. This person was usually the most senior con on the wing and was appointed by the warden. The No. 1 arranged the jobs and dealt with inmate issues. He was like a go-between for inmates who didn't trust the system. Our No. 1 was a bloke called Geordie who happened to be a former Green Jacket like me so, when John moved and I didn't fancy sharing with anyone else, I had a word with Geordie who arranged a job in the servery for me too.

The job wasn't bad and I soon started learning the ropes. Because I was working I was allowed to stay on the wing and life was bearable. I got my own cell with my own toilet so, after months, I could finally have a crap in peace. I was happy – I was in clover. A couple of times a day I put on whites and went down to the kitchens where I helped with the food and wheeled a trolley out to serve the inmates. Prisoners got to choose their weekly meals from a menu. They had choices. I couldn't believe that and was shocked to see how far the authorities bent over backwards to accommodate religious minorities. Everyone had to eat halal meat. It was a real bone of contention and cooks had to use separate equipment for the halal meals. It was all checked by imams who came in regularly to make sure the correct procedures were being followed. It never happened for kosher prisoners; I never saw a rabbi.

There were a lot of divisions in UK prisons based on culture, race and religion, particularly between the Muslim gangs and the rest of the population. There was a lot of pressure on new inmates to convert to Islam, that came from radicals who were not inclined to be friendly. It was really worrying and was the same in all the UK prisons I saw. There was also a lot of resentment because prisoners felt the Muslim inmates got better treatment.

Prisoners were given a classification based on a number of factors, including the severity of the crime they are accused of, their likelihood of absconding, their danger to the public and other prisoners and their behaviour in prison. Each category of prisoner has its own rules. Category A prisoners are either the most dangerous or the most likely to cause trouble and escape. They are required to wear harlequin suits when moved around, they have to be moved on their own and they have to be accompanied by three guards. There are specific jails in the UK that can accommodate cat A prisoners. Then there are cat B, C and D. Most prisoners go in to jail as cat C. Cat D prisoners are usually ones who have been jailed for minor crimes or who are at the end of their sentence and are being prepared for release. Most cat D's go to open prisons and are allowed outside for work placements and home visits.

I was charged with theft so I went in to Norwich as a regular cat C but was hoping I'd be downgraded to a D and get sent to an open prison. I had to go to court every now and then for formal hearings and I was asked to plead. I had discussed the heist with my legal team and explained how I had been forced into it. My barrister advised me that I should plead not guilty because duress was a legitimate defence. The Crown Prosecution Service (CPS), however, had assumed all along that because I volunteered to come back to the UK, I was going to plead guilty. When I didn't I could see the shock on the judge's face. It threw the cat among the pigeons. The police didn't have any evidence to counter a defence of duress; they'd never bothered to interview me formally so didn't know the facts. They didn't really have a case against me and suddenly they needed enough solid evidence to hand to the CPS to justify a trial. In the 20 years since the crime, they had done nothing and they had nothing. I was taken back to Norwich and immediately Suffolk police force went into panic mode. They flew people out to the US to piece together a case and ran around like lunatics trying to gather evidence.

A day after my plea I was on the wing talking to one of the screws when a senior prison officer came up to me and told me to go back to my cell. I did as I was told and he followed me in. I actually thought he was coming to take me to be interviewed by police after the plea as I hadn't been questioned and was never asked for a statement. Instead he said, 'You have been identified as a possible cat A. Pack your gear up, we're taking you to solitary while the bosses decide what to do with you.'

I frowned. 'Cat A? I was hoping for cat D, what's happening?' Cat A prisoners had a much harder time. They were moved every month. Their cells were searched each week and they were strip-searched regularly. All their visitors were vetted and had to be interviewed by police. They had to provide a list of people they wanted to call who were all vetted too. Unvetted visits were conducted through glass and all calls were monitored.

The screw shrugged apologetically. He knew as well as I did there was something devious going on.

I was taken to the solitary wing and my clothes were taken from me. In their place I was given a pair of pyjamas and a green-and-white harlequin jumpsuit. I had a radio instead of a TV. 'You'll be allowed out twice a day to walk around the yard on your own. Make sure you wear the suit when you come out.'

Later that day one of the wardens confirmed that I was to be classified as a cat A. 'We don't have the facilities to hold cat A prisoners here,' she said, 'so we'll have to arrange to move you.'

I remonstrated with her. 'I'm in for theft. It's a C, possibly a D. They must have made a mistake. I'm certainly not a cat A.'

She understood but she had her orders. 'Look, I'll speak to the Home Office and see what's happening. I'm sure it'll all be sorted out by tomorrow and you'll be back on wing. Just sit tight here for a night.'

But it wasn't a night. The next day came and went. I was supposed to have a visit from David, my brother, that weekend but couldn't see him or tell him where I was. I disappeared into the system. Nothing happened over the weekend. I was left in limbo. Then on Monday morning the door opened and three officers came in. 'You're being transferred to a cat A prison,' one of them said. There was no small talk. They were serious and business-like.

'What do you mean? Where am I going?' I asked.

'We can't tell you,' one said.

'Belmarsh,' I said.

He looked shocked. 'I didn't tell you that,' he said.

'I know you didn't. It's written on the lanyard around your neck, you muppet,' I answered. I shook my head, put my suit on and was marched out to a waiting van and taken to one of the country's most notorious lock-ups.

CHAPTER 20

BANG-UP

The van trundled around the M25 and I looked out the small window above my head at a country I barely recognised. I was in the back of another Serco prison transport with no idea of where I was heading. When I left the UK, Belmarsh was only just being built, I didn't really know what it was. I'd heard people mention it in Norwich and assumed by the way they talked that it was hardcore.

My attention wandered and I gazed at the strange country we were travelling through. We got stuck in traffic on the QEII bridge that spanned the Thames near London between Dartford and Thurrock, a crossing that I'd never seen before. Everything looked crowded and small. Even the people looked smaller in their little hatchbacks. I felt like I no longer belonged in the country I was captive in. It wasn't the nation of my youth. There were too many cars and too many people packed together. It felt claustrophobic. The route took us through Essex and past all my old stomping grounds in east London. I was gobsmacked. In 20 years, multiculturalism and immigration had completely changed the face of the area. I know some people will find that observation uncomfortable but it was a fact and it was the thing that I noticed more than anything. When I left, there were no halal butchers and takeaways, there were no sari shops or neon signs in Urdu. Belmarsh was a few miles on from Upton Park, but on the south side of the Thames. The football ground remained and a few stalwart shops and cafes, but the rest was a different land as far as I could see.

The prison was big, featureless and designed along the lines of US jails, its wings spreading out from a central hub. I was taken into reception and immediately it was apparent that security was tight. There was an airport-type X-ray machine that scanned all my possessions. I sat on another X-ray chair and was then taken to a counter where another file was started and I was fingerprinted and swabbed. I was told to stand against a wall and photographed with a card saying 'Category A'. I changed out of the harlequin suit and into the Belmarsh uniform, a maroon sweatsuit and waited on my own in a cell for the obligatory three guards to come and take me to the cat A wing. Each corridor had a locked door at either end. There were gates everywhere. We reached the main accommodation area, which was split into three wings. From the middle I could see down two but there was a steel shutter blocking the other. I found out later that was the nonce wing.

I was taken to the top tier of A wing and shown into my single cell with its TV. I was lost in the system again. I didn't know if anyone knew I was there. The jail felt much more menacing than Norwich and, as a cat A prisoner, I felt immediately that I was looked at differently when I circulated within the wing. The majority of the prison population in any jail are in for minor offences and as a cat A I was in the minority and the other prisoners were wary of me and curious. Generally, cat As stuck out: at visiting times we were made to wear different coloured bibs to the other prisoners so if it kicked off the screws could make a beeline for us first. Cat As take a bit more management and the system places them wherever it has room.

I was put in the junkie's wing to begin with. There were three floors of them, another stark reminder of just how many drug addicts there are in UK prisons. There was only one other cat A, in for money laundering and just given a really long sentence. He was a family man and was a really nice bloke. We got chatting and he explained that in a few weeks he was going to be moved and sent on the 'northern circuit'. I asked what that was and he told me it was system used for cat A prisoners with long sentences. They were sent around the high-security prisons in the north such as Long Lartin, Manchester and Full Sutton. The nonces were sent to Wakefield. This was done to prevent cat As getting used to one prison and one regime. It was a way of reducing the risks of escape and trouble, of always keeping the most risky prisoners on their toes.

Over the weeks I got to know several other cat As and the majority of them were generally more affable than the rest of the population. The shoplifters and junkies all looked, acted and smelled like petty criminals, whereas most of the cat As were better turned out, more intelligent, sociable and were the sort of people I would associate with on the outside. Prison snobbery? Maybe, but it was fact. The money launderers and the blokes who committed offences that took a bit of planning and thought were obviously more interesting and engaging than the little heroin-addict weasels who mugged old ladies or burgled houses. There was certainly a hierarchy in the jail. Groups divided along racial and religious lines and the authorities tried to cater for them all. The chapel had a timetable: some days were for Christian worship, some for Muslims. The Catholics got a slot, the Jewish prisoners had a slot, there was even a weekly Wicca worship.

I started going to chapel on a Sunday, just for something to do and the inmates there tended to be a better class. One bloke came up to me one day and started chatting. He knew me from newspaper reports and asked how I was getting along. He was an older bloke, well spoken, looked a bit foreign. As we talked he mentioned he'd been in Cyprus.

'I was there for a while when I was in the army. I was at the UK forces base there. Where were you?' I asked.

'On the Turkish side, in the north,' he said. He told me his name was Asil. It was only later that I found out who he was. The news about Asil Nadir hadn't made it to the US. He was a Turkish Cypriot tycoon who had been convicted of stealing £29 million from his company, Polly Peck, and given ten years. He was on the run for 17 years and lived in Northern Cyprus – which didn't have an extradition treaty with the UK – until, like me, he returned voluntarily. He was a decent bloke and the next time I saw him was during visiting hours. He had two very glamorous female visitors and you could tell they had lots of money. Later in his sentence he fought to be returned to Turkey to do his bird there. Initially the requests were refused because the Ministry of Justice believed he'd be released early by the Turks. Then, in 2016, his request was finally granted. He went, spent a night in a Turkish jail and was released on probation with no conditions attached.

He was a good example of what I meant about cat As. They were interesting. The main practical advantage of being older and a cat A was that other prisoners left me alone. There were little altercations sometimes and some of the more idiotic cons wanted to make a name for themselves so they looked for fights with cat As but it was never a problem I encountered. I didn't take any shit because I knew I couldn't show weakness but I wasn't exactly a prized scalp so I was left alone.

Mainly, however, being a cat A was a huge inconvenience. Every week the screws came in searched my room and strip-searched me. Some shrugged and apologised, others liked the power trip. 'Strip off, lift your nuts up, Maher,' was a common order. They'd have a poke around down there to make sure I had no contraband hidden under my gonads. It was all designed to be dehumanising and it helped to have a sense of humour about things, otherwise you'd go mad. They had to do it, no one enjoyed it.

Because of its high-security status, there was more lock-in time in Belmarsh. It was called bang-up and a lot of prisoners couldn't handle it. Some of the biggest, toughest ones would crumble when the doors were locked. I, on the other hand, relished it. I felt safer with the door shut. I don't mind associating and I get on well with most other inmates but I preferred people of my choice. Some of those in Belmarsh were arseholes, so I looked forward to bang-up and did a lot of reading. I read everything, I read the whole of *Game of Thrones* before that was made into a TV series. I read *Shōgun*, I read Clive Cussler. I read all genres and anything and everything.

After a couple of weeks, I started work as a cleaner and then moved up to the laundry, which was a better job because it got me out of the cell when everyone else was locked up. I had the run of the place but didn't have to make conversation with anyone. Inmates got their washing done once a week on a set day but I often got approached by people who wanted something extra washed when it wasn't their day. They offered bribes like a Mars bar or cigarettes. I'd refuse. They couldn't understand anyone who didn't live in their world. I wasn't interested though. Getting caught would cause me trouble. I was inside to do my time and get out.

Three weeks after I got sent to Belmarsh I got some great news that lifted my spirits. Debbie and Mark had finally managed to get to the UK. They arrived on 28 August 2012, two days before Debbie would have faced immigration charges. They had had all sorts of problems and were helped by friends and other family. My nephew Tony had been in the States and got in touch when he heard what was happening. He arranged the tickets to get Debbie and Mark back when they finally got their passports.

The bureaucracy they faced had been a Kafkaesque nightmare. In order to get Mark a US passport, Debbie needed a birth certificate with the correct names of his parents. She contacted authorities in Laconia, where Mark had been born, to get our names changed. She was told she could only apply to change the details on a birth certificate in person but she wasn't allowed out of Missouri at the time because she was on bail. Mark himself was underage and couldn't apply for a passport without parental permission, but that took us back to square one: no one legally believed we were his parents because our IDs had been false. Debbie was faced with the awful prospect of being deported and having to leave Mark behind.

Eventually, our friend Brenda stepped in to help. She was friends with one of the judges in Springfield who was really helpful. He got his friends and legal colleagues together in the court house one day for a brainstorm. They realised that the only way to keep the family together was for Debbie to relinquish her legal rights over Mark and assign them to Brenda who would become his legal guardian. She would then be allowed to apply for his passport. Once it was granted and he was in the UK, she would relinquish her role in favour of Debbie. Brenda was happy to oblige.

Even though Mark got his passport completely legally, he

and Debbie were pulled aside by immigration at Gatwick and given a hard time. Home Office officials seized his passport, claiming it had been obtained illegally. They let him in on a six-month visa and Debbie had to get a lawyer to fight for the right for them both to stay in the UK.

In prison I heard many people talk about how their family had been arrested in an effort to increase the pressure on them as inmates, which was bang out of order. It was not a surprise that Norfolk police arrested Debbie, held her for 15 hours and told her she needed to go back whenever they wanted to speak to her. She was put on bail but she has never been charged with anything. They also nicked my sister, who was 63 and a cancer survivor with two walking sticks. Oddly, they never came and questioned me personally.

In the meantime, I continued fighting my cat A status. I was still going for hearings occasionally and I looked up the rules in the Criminal Justice Act and found that theft was not a cat A crime. I lodged a complaint. I discovered that the police had told the prison service I was charged with robbery, which I wasn't. It went on for months. I was issued a case worker, who was good. Eventually, the case went to the Home Office and I won. The ruling came back that I was a cat B prisoner, which was still unfair because I went in as a cat C, so I continued fighting. But the downgrade did give me the chance to have a bit more freedom and thankfully gave my testicles a break too.

I stayed in Belmarsh because my case had been transferred to Southwark Crown Court. I worked in the servery and then got a promotion to tea-boy, which was a good job. I objected to the title and tried to change it to tea-man but that was laughed down by my fellow lags so I invented the title BOS – Beverage Orderly Service. The job allowed me to go off the wing and into the prison officer's restroom to make teas and coffees. I could make myself a brew at the same time. Some prisoners were resentful because I was serving the screws but I didn't care, it was another little bit of freedom and in Belmarsh you took every bit you could get.

I got on well with most of the screws who could see I was trustworthy, no trouble and just wanted to do my time and get out. I worked my way into a job in reception, which was the best job in the prison. Trustees who worked reception spent most days there helping process new arrivals with food, paperwork and laundry. Reception workers got let out every morning before everyone else, worked all day and went back when everyone was locked away. We ate in reception and used the shower there. We had the benefit of being able to use the expensive shower gels that were confiscated from new inmates. It was like having a proper job.

Reception was away from the main prison building and was a more varied place because all sorts of people came through it. There was an X-ray chair there too and it was a constant source of amusement and amazement to see what people were willing to stuff up their backsides to bring inside. The X-ray beeped each time it found something and several times a week I would snigger to myself when I heard it go off. Mainly it was phones and chargers and drugs. A phone would go for £2,000 on the wing so I could see why people who were desperate thought it was a good idea. There were people inside with access to those types of funds on the outside and while no money changed hands on the wing, intermediaries dealt with the transactions.

I worked with a lovely bloke called One-punch Graham. He was a boxing trainer in the army and had unfortunately got in a fight with someone and killed him with one punch. He looked like he wouldn't hurt a fly, thin and wearing glasses. He had been in a pub one day when a bloke started gobbing off. They ended up outside and when the bloke took a swing, Graham hit back. It was just the one punch but Graham knew how to throw it and the bloke went down, hit his head on the floor and never got up. Graham had been in trouble before and got life with a five-year recommendation. Everyone had a story and once I looked past the crimes, there were decent people there. Graham became a good friend and we had a lot of laughs. The reception screws were OK too. One day one of them showed us a plastic tube that was used to store confiscated goods and evidence.

'I've got to show you this because none of us can believe it,' he said. 'We pulled these out of a bloke yesterday.' He pulled out two phones and a charger. 'It's got to be a record,' he said. 'He had all this inside him.'

'Are you shitting me? How the hell did he manage that?' I laughed. The phones were small but it was still an impressive feat.

The months wore on and I looked for things to make

life easier. There were courses for inmates and education opportunities for those who wanted to take them. I was a bit long in the tooth for a City and Guilds in carpentry and didn't fancy basket-weaving but I did sign up for a course called Family Man. It was mainly designed to help people reconnect with their families and build bridges. It was geared towards absent fathers and blokes who hadn't shown a great deal of commitment. In one awful section we had to stand up and sing a song about family values. It was happy-clappy but despite all the bollocks, all of us who took part had a family day every month. The idea was to have our kids in to sit on our knee in a special room so they could see that dad wasn't the monster the courts said he was. Mark was a little too big to sit on my knee at that point and realised that I was a decent human being, but the extra visit sounded like a win. Consequently, the course was well attended. I met a cat A called Alex who was one of the friendliest blokes I could have met. He was always happy, always smiling. He got on well with everyone and never had a bad word about anything. One day he came through reception after a court hearing when I was working and I asked him how his case was going. He said it was OK and I asked him what he was up for. 'Murder,' he said. I gave him the benefit of the doubt; things happen in life and he was such a nice guy.

When he came back after his trial I saw him again. He was smiling as usual and I asked how it went. 'They broke the record,' he said. 'Life with a 47-year rec.' This meant the recommended tariff was 47 years. It was the longest sentence for murder ever given and he was still smiling. I found out later it was something to do with drugs. He was an enforcer and a hit-man who had been sent to kill someone. The target was in bed with a disabled girlfriend and Alex shot them both. The bloke died, the girl survived. Despite the severity of the sentence, Alex remained upbeat and positive, which was just as well because he was looking at a long old stretch.

I also became a prison listener, a voluntary role that was something like being a counsellor. I was trained by the Samaritans. Listeners talked to prisoners who were suicidal. There was a special listening room set aside for privacy. It was actually an old cell of Charles Bronson, famous for being the UK's most dangerous prisoner. There I heard some nightmare stories of lives gone completely off the rails, often for tragic reasons. Some of the inmates had really tough lives – their relationships had broken down, they'd been abused. There were suicides on my wing while I was there. After each one the screws closed the wing down and sent everyone to the cells while they took the poor bastard away. One time a bloke had managed to tie his hands behind his back and tie his legs together and put a pillow case over his head to slowly suffocate himself. While I was there I probably stopped seven or eight people from taking their own lives. It made me realise that there were plenty of people in prison who shouldn't have been there. Many needed help instead of punishment.

After a year, I finally got a date for my trial. The police had been haphazardly scurrying around in the UK gathering evidence and trying to build a case against me. They came up with a load of details that I'd never heard before. They thought I'd gone to the USA using my brother Michael's passport a month after the theft and that the fake passports had been delivered to me in the USA by an accomplice. It sounded like they were clutching at straws. They came up with the names of several people I'd never heard of before, all of whom were arrested and questioned but never charged. They admitted that none of their theories were conclusive and apparently the case against me was within 48 hours of being dismissed. The CPS weighed up whether or not it was in the public interest to prosecute me. There was also a worry that, because the crime had no victims apart from banks and corporations, a jury would sympathise with me rather than with the victims.

If I'd have known all this, things could have been different but at the time I was facing having to make a gamble. The laws regarding sentencing were changing and I was facing a stiffer sentence if I went with the not guilty plea and was found guilty. It was complicated. If I changed my plea and pleaded guilty, I would get a reduction in the sentence. I had served nine months by the time the trial was set which would come off the tariff and I'd get to serve half the sentence outside on licence. It was unlikely I'd get the full sentence of six years because judges didn't like setting maximum benchmarks. So I wasn't looking at much extra jail time; around a year and a few months if I was lucky. If I pleaded not guilty, however, and I was convicted, the changes meant I'd be doing up to nine months extra inside. I knew I could handle just over a year but

I couldn't do any more. I agonised about it and practically the night before the plea I called my lawyer and changed my mind.

In March 2013 I went to Southwark Crown Court and pleaded guilty to theft. The court room was packed with press and there were cameras and TV crews outside. I saw Debbie and Mark in the gallery and gave them a wave. After my plea, the police made a statement and gave their idea about what happened. I sat back and listened to what sounded like a fantastical story of make-believe, concocted in haste. My side didn't mention the duress which I wish we had because it might have countered the cops' version of events. But to be honest, by then I just wanted a quiet life and to be left on my own to get on with my sentence.

The judge retired after the police statement and said he was going to take advice on sentencing. I thought he was going to go outside the guidelines and give me more. He came back and gave me five years. The last thing my side did was ask for the six months I'd spent in the US prison system to come off the sentence. He refused. So that was six months of my life wasted because the authorities in the UK couldn't be bothered to facilitate my extradition. I waved goodbye to my family and trudged back down to the cells before being taken back to Belmarsh. At least it was a day out and I got to put on some smart clothes for a change.

The case was all over the news again and when I was inside people I'd never spoken came up, patted me on the back and asked me about it. Those two common questions were asked again and again. 'How did you do it?', 'Where's the money?'

My answer? 'Read the book.'

I continued to fight my cat B status, arguing that as I started at cat C and was wrongly made an A, by that time I should have been a D. I was also a trusted prisoner and listener and was actually a valuable part of prison society. I was told I couldn't have cat D because there was a confiscation hearing pending. This was another little indignity that the state decided to put on me. When I was arrested the fire brigade pension fund notified the courts that I had money in a fund, which accumulated long before the crime. While I had been in the US I had stopped drawing the pension so it sat in a pot and built up. It was money earned when I was in the brigade and by 2013 it stood at about £58,000. A smarter police force might have frozen my assets but Suffolk never even looked. After my conviction for theft the Home Office started proceedings to recover the money so it could be paid to the victims of my crime – Securicor and its insurance company.

The months went by. Prison life ground on. Every so often something happened that broke the monotony. It wasn't always good. In February 2014, I was in reception when Fusilier Lee Rigby's killers came through. He had been attacked near the Royal Artillery Barracks in Woolwich and his murder had shocked the whole country. Many of the screws and several prisoners were former soldiers and to them the murder was particularly abhorrent. Michael Adebolajo had been given a whole-life term and Michael Adebowale had been jailed for a minimum of 45 years. We'd heard the news on a radio and knew they were coming to Belmarsh because it was high-security and had a AA maximum security unit within it. This had its own gym, it was totally separate and inmates' food was prepared over there so no one could tamper with it.

Graham and I were in reception when one of the guards asked if we could plate up a couple of meals for inmates who had been in court. They needed halal and we were told the guards would take the meal to them. We realised who the food was for, and, while I can't divulge too many details, I can say that they had a really nice meal that day! When they arrived we were put in a room for inmates and locked inside, which had never happened before. There was a glass panel on the door and we saw them come through. After that stories circulated in the prison about them. Apparently one of the screws beat one of them up and the youngest one apparently cried his eyes out all the time and wanted a priest so he could convert to Christianity.

Eventually, I was back in court for my own confiscation hearing and I didn't fight it. The courts decided my pension was the proceeds of crime and it was to be divided between the insurance company and Securicor. I was in jail and potless. I shouldn't moan. I was lucky because I was done under the Criminal Justice Act which was in force at the time of the crime, rather than the Proceeds of Crime Act, under which they can keep coming back at you each time you earn a pound for ever afterwards.

I kept drilling the prison management about my cat D status. One of the governors eventually got behind me and pushed it through. As soon as I reached the heady heights of cat D, I was eligible to move to a cat D prison. I wanted to go to Ford because it was near where Debbie and Mark were renting in Eastbourne and, although there were never any guarantees and prisoners could end up anywhere, when the day came to leave, my colleagues on reception made sure the bus I boarded was going there.

CHAPTER 21

THE FINAL FURLONG

I sat in a parked van outside Ford for an hour wondering what was happening. The inmate who had come in the Serco transport with me had gone in and been processed. I was left in the cell in the van. I'd already spent enough time in security vans for my liking and was anxious to get out. Another 30 minutes went by before a screw put his head through the door and explained there had been a problem and I might have to go back to Belmarsh.

'We've just found out there's a confiscation order against you,' he said.

'It's been done, discharged,' I explained.

'We haven't had the paperwork,' he apologised. Luckily, I had a file of it with me. I had four big bags that I had insisted the solicitor sent me after the case so I told the screw and dug out the relevant document to show him.

HMP Ford was in West Sussex and was a lot easier going that anywhere else I'd been. It consisted of many accommodation huts spread out over a wide area and a row of two-storey blocks ringed by a chain fence that was topped with barbed wire. The prison was low and flat. There was a big, open area in the middle. It was weird initially to see people wandering around. I was told to wait outside and someone would be along to show me where to go and to help me with my bags. Then I was left alone. For a moment it was disorientating. I was out, on my own and there was nothing stopping me turning around and walking out of the front gates.

A couple of prisoners strolled down with a cart, said hello, and told me they would show me to my room.

'A room? Don't you have cells here?' I asked.

They laughed but I'm sure they'd heard it hundreds of times before. They asked where I was from and I told them I had come from Belmarsh. They were impressed, it was very unusual for anyone to go from a cat A prison straight to a cat D. I beat the record from A to D.

The prison was split in two and had a road running through the middle of it. Prisoners were free to walk through the gate, cross the road at the zebra crossing and walk to the other side. Or they could walk up the road to Ford railway station and go.

My accommodation was a double cell, which I wasn't too happy about but the welcome party explained that there was a waiting list for the single cells. Everyone wanted them and it took about nine months to get a cell with your own key and a door you could lock yourself. The huts had showers and a kitchenette with a kettle and a microwave. All of the prisons in the UK provided kettles for inmates which I found odd after the USA. I knew a kettle could be used as a weapon and I had heard about prisoners boiling hot water and sugar up to throw over enemies. The concoction stuck to the skin and burned like napalm.

Initially, I was put in a hut with a bloke who was OK. He was a smoker and it was a non-smoking hut, but they were popular because they were cleaner. He was hooked on *Big Brother*, which I hated so we had to work out a rota. He'd get excited about eviction nights. It was on after lock-up and I had to sit there and watch it with him. Each night at a certain time we were supposed to stay in our huts but in practice there was nothing stopping us going out and walking around or going into someone else's hut. When *Big Brother* bloke went another bloke came and I told him that he could watch what he wanted on the television but after 8pm it was mine. He was a big soccer fan and was unhappy with the arrangement but as the senior inmate I got to call the shots. We didn't get on that well.

There were a lot of inmates who were in for petty offences. The second bloke I shared with was in for shoplifting and another bloke in the next hut was serving a ten-week sentence for motoring offences. In my view they shouldn't have sent people like that to Ford, which was designed for prisoners who had been in the system for a long time and needed a halfway house in which to get used to life back in the outside world. There was friction between long-term cat Ds and the petty criminals and junkies who didn't need the day visits or work-release schemes because they'd only been inside for a few months. The long-term lags needed the rehabilitation and my argument was that I needed it because I hadn't been in the UK for 20 years. I needed time to adjust to what was a completely alien country for me.

There were different jobs inside the prison; some people were cleaners, some did gardening in the market garden which then sold produce on. For a time, I worked in the medical dispensary as an orderly and then I signed up for a work-release scheme. There were a small number of jobs on the outside, mainly in charity shops. Vacancies were advertised on a noticeboard in the prison. I eventually got a job with the shoe repair and key-cutting chain Timpsons. I started earning a wage which was a help, although the prison service took half of it. Throughout my time inside, Debbie had been providing money for me and the whole process was costly for her because she had to travel to visit me.

Timpsons had a long-standing partnership with the prison service and was one the UK's main providers of prisoner work-placement and training. It ran a training facility inside a prison in Tunbridge Wells in Kent in which inmates learned how to repair shoes, watches and phones and cut keys. Any firm entering into a work scheme with prisoners needed to be thoroughly vetted and it was a long process. After expenses, I ended up taking home around £20 a week. After training I was then allowed out to work in a shop in Brighton. Prisoners were expected to make their own way to their outside jobs so for the first time in over two decades I found myself using UK public transport. There was an 8pm curfew and every day it was a panic to get back in time. I wasn't much of a shoe-repairer but the thing I really struggled with was dealing with the public, who were mainly rude.

After a few months I was given a branch to manage in Lancing, near Debbie. It was a hut outside a supermarket that I opened up in the morning. One day I noticed that one of the doors was slightly ajar. When I got inside, the till was missing and the safe had been busted open. I called the area manager, who got the police. I assumed I'd get a hard time. The cops did a search of the area and found the empty till.

'We'll dust for prints,' one of them said.

'That might be interesting,' I said.

'Why?' he asked.

'It'll have my prints and when you run them through the system they'll be flagged up.'

'I thought I recognised you,' said the copper. 'Aren't you Fast Eddie?' I nodded and the copper joked: 'Are you sure it wasn't you?' before he asked for an autograph.

'It's a bit beneath him,' answered the area manager.

After six weeks I became eligible for releases. At first I was allowed to meet up with Debbie but was not allowed to go home and had to back at 8pm. Later I qualified for five-day home visits, after my chosen residence was checked by the probation service. There were often a lot of obstructions in the way for inmates who had legal rights to make visits but who found it overly bureaucratic trying to get them.

My first town leave was scary. I met Debbie and we walked into a Primark but I immediately wanted to get out straight away. There were too many people. Everywhere was crowded and no one respected personal space. It was very uncomfortable. People were not as I remembered them; the politeness and manners I remembered had gone and even the old people were rude. I couldn't believe what people wore. In the US only women wore three-quarter length trousers. Leggings were new to me – in the US they were tights and people wore skirts or shorts over them. A lot of the older women in the UK also seemed to dress like 20-year-olds. Debbie and I were shocked. All the young girls looked like clones and everyone had tattooed flesh on display. It wasn't the country I left or one I'd choose to live in.

It got harder in Ford as my release date came nearer; I just wanted to get out, but had to stay in and mix with people I didn't want to be with. I just wanted to get home to be with my family and support them because they were having trouble. Mark finished school and did really well. He passed 14 GCSEs and applied for a place in college, which he got. But he still didn't have a passport because the US one that had been seized at Gatwick had never been returned. His college refused to accept him because he didn't have citizenship and agreed to defer the place for a year while he got his status in order. Debbie started the process for him. He was British by descent because Debbie and I were British. The whole thing should have been a formality and he was entitled to a UK passport. However, even though the authorities knew the story and they knew who we were, they still said there was no legal proof that Mark was our son because we used false names to register his birth. Debbie argued and in the end the only solution was for her to take a DNA test to prove to the Home Office that she was Mark's mother. Debbie herself couldn't work for a long time, even though she wanted to. It was easier for me than it was for her. People don't realise how hard it is for the families of prisoners. My basic needs were provided for, but Debbie had to look after her and Mark on her own.

Towards the end of my sentence I got a single cell which came with a key. It was a relief to have my own space. Ford had its problems and the population there was hard to fathom. Nowhere was the juxtaposition between prisoners intent on making a life for themselves and petty criminals who would be back inside two weeks after release more apparent. There were some really thick people in Ford. In an open prison it was easier to bring things in. Phone-smuggling was a problem but I could never understand why anyone would take the risk in an open prison. Legal highs were also a huge issue. There were loads of inmates bringing them in. They were called things like 'Bath Salts' or 'Spice' and were used as currency. People took them and went doolally. They found one bloke frothing at the mouth and trying to swim a puddle. It was deadly stuff and the junkies always overdid it. I regretted going there in the end.

After just over a year I got out, in February 2015. My release date had been set from the date of sentencing but, up to the day I got out I didn't believe it would happen. I assumed they'd find something else to hang on me and keep me inside. I didn't trust the system. I had got all my things in order. There was more paperwork, of course – I signed forms to confirm I had handed my library books back. I packed my stuff into black binbags and the next morning I packed up my bedding and handed it back to reception, waited until 9am and, finally, I was told I could go. I walked out under licence to Debbie who was waiting for me. There were a few tears of relief, but no parties or celebrations. It was enough just to be with my family. Being away from them had always been the hardest part. We'd been on the run together as a team for 20 years, my freedom was that we were back together.

EPILOGUE

FREEDOM, OF SORTS

So, there you have it, finally, the answers from the horse's mouth, the gospel according to Fast Eddie. The true story of how a normal bloke from East London managed to deprive the UK's biggest security firm of over £1 million in cash and then evade capture for 19 years... I almost got away with it.

I started thinking about writing my story when I was in prison because the questions kept coming. And when I heard the inaccurate official version at my trial and saw how much interest there had been in my story, I started putting pen to paper and I wrote the first pages. The how-did-you-do-it and the where's-the-money questions never went away, even after I was released.

Following the trial, when I disappeared into the prison system, Debbie was still hounded by the press. One bloke, the epitome of an unscrupulous hack, gained her confidence then published a load of stuff without her permission. Eventually she was contacted by a PR agent who helped her to field off the unwanted attention.

When I left Ford on licence, word got out quickly that I was a free-ish man. Someone must have tipped off the press. I had continued to work for Timpson and, in the first week I was out, I was leaving the house to go to work and, as I was getting in the car, two men approached me. 'Eddie, Eddie, can I just ask a couple of questions?' one of them begged. The other had a camera and was snapping happily away at me.

'Sorry, I don't have time. I'm on my way to work,' I replied and quickly got in my car and drove away.

They followed for a while and then lost interest. The next day the story that I was out of prison and working was in one of the papers and, according to the writer, I'd said that I had done my time, rather than that I didn't have time.

While it wasn't remotely enjoyable, prison did teach me some valuable lessons. You can't judge a book by its cover. Just because someone is in jail, they are not automatically a bad person. There are many levels of criminality and many people in jail are there because others have failed them. Many people need help, not incarceration. As far as I could tell there was no rehabilitation in prison, it was a system purely used for punishment and it failed a lot of people who would have benefited from training and education. There were some people caught in the cycle of prison and re-offending and they spent their lives choking up the system, costing the taxpayer money. If they were identified and given a purpose everyone would have benefited. I met one bloke in Belmarsh one day who was only a kid, in his mid-twenties. Like a lot of lags he was talking about what he was going to do when he got out. He was excited about going to a McDonald's drive-through. He'd never seen one because he'd been in so long. He went to jail as a juvenile and stayed there except for a few releases during which he re-offended immediately and was caught. I doubt he ever got out because, despite the desire to eat a Big Mac in a car, people like him were institutionalised. There were people who just wanted to be in closed conditions and couldn't deal with the demands of normal life. In Ford, I found that a lot of the long-timers feared getting out. Several of them walked out, over-stayed curfew and then walked down to Lewes police station and handed themselves in, knowing that having absconded, they would not be allowed back in an open prison.

My release was a culture shock for me. Even though I had some time to get used to the UK during my home visits the changes still took me by surprise. There were little things that niggled. When I first started driving again I couldn't understand why motorbikes tried to overtake me in my lane and expected me to pull over. That was illegal when I left the UK but everyone was doing it. And there were bigger changes too.

People were more aggressive, no one got out of your way, everyone was on a phone or tapping on a screen, no one said 'Please', 'Thank you' or 'Sorry'. Manners had gone. Everyone seemed depressed and loved to talk about it. There were no stiff upper lips, everyone had a problem and they wanted the world to know. There was no respect for the things that used to be valued. Everyone was drunk and town centres were no-go zones at night. Everyone was either pissed or high and the waft of cannabis could be smelled everywhere.

I couldn't get used to the different languages that were spoken. Down every street I heard conversations I didn't understand. Twenty years previously, it was unusual to hear another language. Now there was certainly more racial tension and people didn't seem tolerant of each other. The divisions between cultures and races were as clear on the outside as they were in prison. If you talked about it, you got accused of being racist and I was not sure I wanted to live in a country where making valid observations about change was frowned upon. It seemed to me that, in the UK I was released into, people were only allowed to think certain ways and were not allowed to question. That was fascism. In the US people knew their rights and defended their freedoms. Civil liberties in the UK were weak and constantly eroded. Speed cameras, facial recognition software, CCTV and the government and its agencies were always prying into lives.

Change isn't always good and the changes I noticed were not for the better. It wasn't a joyful homecoming. Seeing how much the country had gone to the dogs soured my release and made me feel like I was in another prison without walls. The only good thing I could see was that the country had become a cheaper place to live. People moaned about being skint but prices were either the same as when I left or only marginally higher. Everyone seemed to have accumulated a lot of stuff in the interim and everyone seemed to have a new car.

The UK didn't feel like home any longer and I felt stateless. I suspected that as soon as we could, we would start looking to leave the UK and I encouraged Mark, who had dual citizenship, to get back to the US as soon as he could because the prospects and lifestyle were much better there for young people.

Mark was brilliant throughout everything. He could have easily gone the other way. Any kid would have rebelled against it all but Mark was a dream. At school, he did very well and he settled into college and university, made friends and made the most of things. We had always tried to bring him up as a law-abiding citizen and Debbie had taught both the boys to respect the law and, if they were in trouble, to go to a cop. After her own arrest and following the treatment she received, she's now more likely to tell them to run for the hills instead.

Lee returned to the UK too, got a job and sorted himself out. The arrest and subsequent events were difficult for him but he was not a quitter and he turned himself around.

Debbie got a part-time job and made a home for us before Mark left for university. She dealt with so much of the crap and fallout but still came out the other side the strong, positive person she always was.

Things didn't work out so well for Jessica. The £100,000 blood money she was expecting apparently never materialised. I heard that although she hired a lawyer to help her claim the reward, she only got a small fraction because the small print stipulated that the reward had been offered on condition that my arrest led to recovery of the stolen money. And that as we all know, was long gone.

I was released on licence with no restrictions, apart from the requirement that if I wanted to stay somewhere overnight other than my home, I was supposed to tell my probation officer where I was going. I was not allowed to travel out of the country and I was only allowed to take a job that the probation service authorised.

Which brings us up to date.

I've realised that there is so much more to my life than a stolen van. Rightly or wrongly, that moment defines me for the people I meet but there are so many incidents and stories beyond it. I've been a Las Vegas gambler, a trucker, a corporate suit. I've saved lives, I've pulled people from fires and off mountains and talked people back from the brink of suicide. How do you condense 11 years in the fire brigade in one of the busiest fire stations in the world into a chapter or cut down the unique viewpoint of having experienced jails in the UK and the US into only a few thousand words? It is a story of immense breadth. There is so much more to tell and mine has not been a life wasted by a single crime.

People have been fascinated for 20 years because, if they are honest, I did something everybody wanted to do or would have done given half the chance. Most people give me a wink and wish me luck. I've never come across anyone who pointed a finger and condemned me. Today you have people online who steal ten times as much as I did at the touch of a button. It wasn't long after my own indiscretion that some much bigger crimes were carried out. My own, in comparison, now seems almost parochial.

In the end, I was never questioned by the police and was surprised at how easy it was not to get caught. I was always waiting for the knock on the door. Now, if plod wants to know my side of the story, they can read the book.

So do I regret what I did? Of course, I regret the effect it has had on my family but if I hadn't done it, they might not be here. Even if the gangsters hadn't gone through with their threats, we might not have had Mark and I would probably have ended up in a dead-end job somewhere. My life wasn't going anywhere when it happened. Instead I've done things people dream of. So, regrets? No. I've hopefully paid my dues and probably given more back to society than I've taken.

And what does the future hold? Watch this space. People will inevitably have more questions and I'll keep telling my stories but one thing is for sure. I don't plan on hanging around. The first chance I get, me and the family will be off. Old habits die hard.

ACKNOWLEDGEMENTS

Thank you to Brenda Morris who helped and supported us when everything was turning sour. She has been a lifesaver and true friend to Debbie and me through some very dark days.

Thank you to Denise Palmer Davies at Borne Media and Kelly Ellis and the team at Blink for all the help and work they have put in to make this possible. Denise is not only a good agent but a friend to Debbie and I who has helped us put this together.

And, finally, thanks to Nick Harding without whom this would have been a very long and laboured project. Working with me through your wedding day and honeymoon was above and beyond! Thanks, Nick, possibly the last person in the world still using shorthand...